FAMILIES EXPLORING FAITH

A Parents' Guide to the Older Adolescent Years

Audrey Taylor
and Joe Taylor

THE WORLD OF
DON BOSCO
MULTIMEDIA

NEW ROCHELLE, NY

Families Exploring Faith: A Parents' Guide to the Older Adolescent Years is published as part of the Catholic Families Series—resources to promote faith growth in Families.
Materials available for parish and diocesan leaders, parents and families

Available titles:

For leaders and ministers:
Families and Young Adults
Families and Youth
Families and Young Adolescents
Growing in Faith: A Catholic Family Sourcebook
Media, Faith, and Families: A Parish Ministry Guide
Rituals for Sharing Faith: A Resource for Parish Ministers
Faith and Families: A Parish Program for Parenting in Faith Growth

For parents and families:
Families Nurturing Faith: A Parents' Guide to the Preschool Years
Families Sharing Faith: A Parents' Guide to the Grade School Years
Families Experiencing Faith: A Parents' Guide to the Young Adolescent Years
Families Encouraging Faith: A Parents' Guide to the Young Adult Years
Media, Faith, and Families: A Parents' Guide to Family Viewing
Family Rituals and Celebrations

The Catholic Families Series is a publishing project of Don Bosco Multimedia and the Center for Youth Ministry Development

Families Exploring Faith: A Parents' Guide to the Older Adolescent Years
©1992 Salesian Society, Inc. / Don Bosco Multimedia
475 North Ave., P.O. Box T, New Rochelle, NY 10802

Library of Congress Cataloging-in-Publication Data

Families Exploring Faith: A Parents' Guide to the Older Adolescent Years
/   Joe and Audrey Taylor
p. cm. — Catholic Families Series
Includes bibliographical references.
        1. Family life 2. Religious development
            I. Taylor, Joe. II. Taylor, Audrey.
ISBN 0-89944-254-4 $6.95

Design and Typography by Sally Ann Zegarelli, Long Branch, NJ 07740

Printed in the United States of America

6/92   9 8 7 6 5 4 3 2 1

PREFACE

FAMILIES EXPLORING FAITH: A PARENTS' GUIDE TO THE OLDER ADOLESCENT YEARS

A quick look at the family section of your local bookstore will reveal dozens of books about parenting. What you probably will not find among these titles is a book about parenting and faith growth. To fill this void, we have created five books which help parents of children from the pre-school years through the young adult years nurture the faith growth of their children. These new titles are part of the Catholic Families Series published by Don Bosco Multimedia.

Older adolescents are caught up in the challenges presented by new ways of thinking, an expanded circle of contacts and friends, greater autonomy and the need to redefine relationships. But they still need your concern and care. You can continue to have an influence on their faith and values, and grow with them in the process.

Families Exploring Faith is specifically designed for parents of older adolescents. It provides you with an understanding of the unique characteristics of older adolescents and their families at this stage of life. It outlines the possibilities for sharing faith with older adolescents through the authors' personal stories and through specific strategies and activities. It also suggests ways that you can continue your growth in faith.

Our hope is to promote opportunities for families with older adolescents to continue the faith sharing and faith growth which began in childhood. We hope you find the stories, insights and ideas a source of support and encouragement as you continue parenting.

ABOUT THE AUTHORS

Audrey Taylor is Director of Youth Ministry at St. Theresa Parish in Palatine, IL and Adolescent Catechesis Consultant for Chicago's Archdiocesan CYO. **Joe Taylor** is Director of Campus Ministry at Loyola Prep in Chicago. Joe and Audrey have undergraduate and graduate degrees from Loyola University of Chicago and Masters degrees in Pastoral Ministry from Loyola's Institute of Pastoral Studies. Audrey has created and facilitated parent-teen evenings and retreats throughout the Archdiocese of Chicago. Audrey and Joe are the parents of seven children, currently spanning adolescence and young childhood.

CONTENTS

1

PARENTING FOR FAITH GROWTH TODAY

WHY FAMILIES NEED FAITH

As every good parent knows, parenting involves much more than providing basic food and shelter, education and health care. Parenting is also about loving and caring, building self-esteem and a sense of values. Effective parenting helps children understand how they relate to others and what they can do to make the world a better place for themselves and for all people.

Parenting is a shared task. Despite all the different shapes that families come in today—single-parent and two-parent, blended and extended—the challenge of parenting continues to be shared across generations and across family lines. Grandparents, aunts and cousins share in the task, as do special friends who have become "family" for us in a different way. People of faith proclaim that God is also an active partner with them in their job of parenting.

Faith provides family members with shared beliefs and values to guide their life together and to direct their involvement beyond the family circle. Faith values nurture the family's well-being and provide it with the criteria needed to weigh and evaluate the many messages that come its way each day. Faith proclaims, for example, that every person is endowed by God with dignity and blessed with a unique mix of gifts and talents. These gifts and talents, in turn, are meant to be shared with others. This vision of personhood calls families to recognize, nurture and celebrate the uniqueness of each family member. It also calls families to recognize their interdependence with others and to share the talents and gifts nurtured in family life with others in their community and world. As simple as this faith value seems, it often stands in sharp contrast to societal messages that judge people in light of what they have or that promote isolation from others who seem, at least at first glance, to be different from us.

As parents model faith values at home and in the community, nurture a sense of dignity and uniqueness in their children and encourage family members to share their talents with others, they join with God in the sacred task of building a world based on gospel values. Children, in turn, take what they have learned and practiced at home and carry it into the world, guaranteeing a new generation committed to creating a world based on gospel values.

Faith serves, as well, as a source of comfort and strength for parents, assuring them that they are not alone in the task of parenting and providing them with a special Friend to whom they can turn for direction and support. As parents join with their God in the task of parenting, they come to realize that there are no social, geographical or educational barriers to good parenting. Good parenting does not depend upon a high hourly wage, a prestigious address or the number of degrees after a person's name. You don't have to be a biological parent to develop a strong family life. You can be an adoptive parent, a single parent, a parent of healthy or handicapped children. Good parenting is possible for all people who trust enough in themselves, in the other members of their families and in their God.

Faith provides people with the values and vision needed to live life fully. Families need faith to survive and thrive in today's world. Our challenge in this book is to offer you and your family practical insights and strategies for developing a meaningful faith life.

KEYS TO EFFECTIVE PARENTING

Before we begin this book on parenting for faith growth and turn to the descriptions and suggestions offered by our authors, it will be important to look at the adventure of parenting today and what we mean by parenting for faith growth.

As noted above, the key to effective parenting lies within you. Your drive to make your family the best that it can be need not be blocked by your particular life circumstances. To be sure, your path may be more winding and littered than some, but effectiveness in parenting is an internal quality, not easily squashed by external conditions. It is a desire to make the most of yourself and your family, whatever your talents or situation.

What do we know about effective parenting? Who can we turn to for advice? One of the best sources for our wisdom about parenting is to turn to other parents. In *Back to the Family*, Dr. Ray Guarendi gathered the shared wisdom of one hundred of America's happiest and most effective families. He shares the following thoughts on what makes families effective:[1]

1. **A strong home life does not depend upon a parent's education, occupation, ethnicity or social status.** Neither is it limited to biological parents, two-parent homes or a low-stress

existence. Effective parenting and a strong home life are not the product of external causes but are born internally. They evolve from commitment, from determination to build upon your family's strengths, regardless of what factors may be pulling against you.

2.   Successful parents are not all products of successful childhoods. While many parents knew upbringings filled with positive examples from which to anchor their own parenting, others have lived through childhoods best described as cold, abusive or even traumatic. Parents who have risen far above their childhoods are living proof that, contrary to some experts' opinions, the quality of your past does not put a ceiling on the quality of your present as a parent or as a person.

3.   Effective parents are not perfect or even close to perfect. They wrestle with worries, insecurities and guilts all parents feel. They don't have all the answers, endless patience or perfect children. Their lives reveal that skillful parenting is not inborn. It is developed over time, along with a healthy acceptance of one's imperfections. Better parenting results from recognizing our limits and working to overcome them or live with them.

4. Good parents love to parent. They've experienced the challenges and fears inherent to childrearing and remain grateful for the opportunity to be parents. Lifestyles and priorities can change radically with the decision to raise children. Responsible parents accept this reality, even welcome it.

5.   Common sense and good judgment form the foundation for sound parenting decisions. Having discovered that no one right way exists for handling any situation, effective parents strive for self-confidence. It leads to more decisive parenting and more secure children. Childrearing is a never-ending process. It is drawing upon the knowledge and experience of others—children, parents and experts. The willingness to learn from others is indispensable to better parenting, but ultimately you must judge for yourself what will work for your family, based upon your values and unique circumstances.

6.   A parent's personality has far more influence on her childrearing than being aware of all the latest childrearing trends. Work to become a better person and your parenting will automatically improve.

7.   Wise parents are open to guidance from their children. Children are natural teachers of childrearing. They know us well—in many ways, better than anyone else does. Since they are with us every day, they are ready and able to give us feedback on our technique. Living mirrors, they reflect back at us who we are, what we act like, what we sound like. Lessons most basic to successful parenting are taught by children:

- *Show your love.* At the heart of all quality parenting is unconditional love. No matter what our children do, our love for them will never cease. Unconditional love is the basis for every parenting decision and action. It is the driving force behind all discipline.

- *Teach through example; practice what you preach.*

- *Listen before you talk.*

- *Look through a child's eyes.* Children do not see parenthood through the eyes of parents.

8.   A relaxed parent is a better parent. How fully we enjoy our children is directly related to two factors: a relaxed attitude toward childrearing and being prepared for the inevitable rough times that every parent faces. There are ways to parent more calmly right now. Enjoyable childrearing begins with accepting several parenting facts of life. These are truths at the very heart of parenthood.

- *Don't try to be a perfect parent.* Undeserved anxiety and guilt will follow.

- *Don't fear mistakes.* They are necessary for maturation. Good parents become better through mistakes.

- *Parent in the present.* Second guessing yourself or dwelling on the uncertain future will erode your confidence and ability to give your best to your children today.

- *Expect that your children will misunderstand and dislike you at times.* That is a reality of responsible parenthood.

- *Laugh whenever and wherever you can during child-rearing.* Humor helps maintain perspective and eases anxiety.

9.   Spiritual beliefs are a dominant presence in strong families. Faith in a Creator and in living by God's guidelines provide values which nurture each member's personal growth and thereby the family's. Spirituality fosters parenting through example, the most durable parenting. It is a source of comfort and strength, enabling parents to call upon a supreme authority for wisdom and direction.

10.   There are no shortcuts to strong family life. A parent must invest time. Dedication means a willingness to give quantity time, which is necessary for quality time. Time provides the framework for all elements of family success—communication, discipline, values. Making family a priority fosters a child's self-esteem and sense of belonging. Nothing is more precious to a child than the presence of a parent.

11.   Competent parents concentrate on mastering the basics of communication. A few good principles guide them:

- *Talk less at children and listen more to them.* Attentive silence is the simplest way to evoke a child's feelings.

- *Become sensitive to children's prime times to talk.* Arrange them or be present when they occur. They are windows into their thoughts.

- *Affection is continuous communication.* It is love without words. Strong families know the binding power of affection.

- *Whenever possible, allow children a voice in family decisions.* While in most cases, parents retain the final say, merely being consulted makes a child feel an integral part of the family.

12. Responsible parents expect much of their children and of themselves. Their attitude is, "Success is not measured against others but against yourself. Striving for your personal best is a success." Parents counsel:

- *Insist on your children's full effort in academics.* It is their future.

- *The family home is everyone's home, so make it everyone's responsibility,* down to the youngest members.

- *Judge children's capabilities—social, emotional, personal—and expect them to live up to them.* Don't allow them to live down to the norm.

13. Strong parents believe in strong discipline begun young. They are willing to exert whatever effort is necessary to discipline their children today so life won't discipline them tomorrow. The firmest parent, if loving, is a more gentle teacher than the world. For a child's sake, parents need the will to discipline. The best discipline is motivated by unconditional love, love that is unaffected by a child's misbehavior. Good disciplinarians focus most on what children do right, not wrong. They emphasize the positive. Not only does this make for less discipline, it enhances a child's self image. By their nature, children test limits and want more than is healthy for them. Loving parents are not afraid to say no. They draw clear boundaries within which a child is free to operate.

The mechanics of effective discipline are summarized by the three C's: calm, consistency and consequences. Calm discipline works more quickly and leads to less regrettable behavior from everyone. Consistency is predictability. It enables children to understand and accept the results of their actions. Consequences, not words, are the basic tools of discipline.

14. Strong families rely on simple, clear-cut home rules enforced by consequences. They derive some of their stability from house rules. Established according to a family's needs and goals, rules make for a more content household. The content of the rules changes as the family evolves, but their purpose remains the constant: to promote mutual respect, responsibility and a more pleasant environment for everyone.

Refined to its most basic elements, successful parenting is unconditional love, commitment, teaching by example and the will to discipline. Effective parenting is an attainable reality. Build upon the essentials, and no level of family success is beyond your reach. In this book we will be encouraging you to utilize these ingredients of effective parenting by suggesting practical insights and skills for parenting young adults.

THE FAMILY AS A LIVING SYSTEM

No human being grows in a vacuum. To be human is, by definition, to be interdependent, to rely on others for the support and assistance needed to grow to full life. No place is this more apparent than in the life of the family. Family members depend upon one another and have a tremendous impact on one another's growth. Change and growth in any family member's life automatically impacts all other family members. If a major change occurs in the life of a single family member, all members are forced to adjust to the change. This can entail adjustments in the relationships among individual family members or a recasting of what it means to be family together.

Researchers use the term "system" to describe the organic relationship that exists between individual family members and the family as a whole. You may remember from high school science classes that living organisms and their environments function as a system. All living systems attempt to maintain *equilibrium* or balance. When a change takes place that upsets this balance, the system responds by doing something to restore the equilibrium that existed previously.

The family is a system, too—a system in which relationships change in response to the changing needs and concerns of family members and in response to changes in the family's relationship with the larger society. And like other systems, families attempt to maintain a sense of equilibrium in their relationships. Certain understandings develop regarding roles, rules, relationships and responsibilities in the family. These understandings form the system by which the family operates. Often times, families are unaware of how these roles, rules, relationships and responsibilities affect their entire life as a family.

The tendency for family systems to try to maintain their established patterns of behavior is challenged from time to time by changes to which they must adapt. These changes can be a regular part of the family's growth and development. The birth of the first child causes an imbalance in the family system of the couple, often making many of the former roles, rules, relationships and responsibilities unworkable. The arrival of adolescence brings with it periods of imbalance as formerly accepted roles, rules, relationships and responsibilities are questioned by the adolescent. During these life transitions it is *healthy* for family roles, rules, relationships and responsibilities to change, for through such changes families adjust to the changes and restore a new balance to the system.

Sometimes these changes are brought about by major events in the life of the family, such as the loss of a parent through death or divorce or the remarriage of parents resulting in a new blended family. The members of a family must find ways to reorganize and reestablish workable roles, rules, relationships and responsibilities in light of these major life events. Such changes often result in longer periods of imbalance as the family system seeks to adjust to the changes and establish a new balance. Making changes during these major events is difficult, but it is *healthy*. Families need to adjust to the new situation they face and restore a new balance to the system. Only in this way can the family feel comfortable again.

At other times, you as the parent may wish to make a change in the family by introducing new ways of relating, new patterns of family living, new rules, new practices, etc. In this book we introduce you to a variety of ways to share faith with your children. You may want to use many of these new ideas in your family. Be aware that family members often resist change, not because the changes are bad, but because change is upsetting. It causes anxiety. When a family establishes its balance, members are comfortable with the status quo. Anything new, even if positive, will likely be resisted, and a subtle message of "change back" will be communicated. Change requires at least three steps: the change itself, the family's reaction to the change and dealing with the family's reaction to the change. By understanding how your family system works (what the roles, rules, relationship patterns and responsibilities are), you can be prepared for your family's reaction. For example, you can identify what needs to change in order to introduce the idea, involve family members in deciding and planning for the change, keep communication lines open during the change, suggest that they try the new idea for a specific length of time and then evaluate, etc.

HOW FAMILIES GROW

Today it has become commonplace to talk about the changes we experience throughout our lives. We are aware of the differing life tasks and characteristics of childhood, adolescence, young adulthood, middle adulthood and later adulthood. Each of these "stages" or times of life brings with it new challenges and important life tasks to accomplish. In a family both children and parents are experiencing their own individual journeys.

We may not be as fully aware that the family as a unit or system has important life tasks to address and needs and functions to fulfill. A family in its "infancy" is different from a family in its "adolescence." Like individuals, families move through a life cycle, a family life cycle—that is, various stages in which new issues arise and different concerns predominate. During the first years of marriage, for example, families focus nearly all their energy on establishing a household, finding suitable employment and strengthening the marital relationship. During the child-bearing stage, the family's concerns shift to taking care of their young children. Families are likely to have higher medical expenses, more debts in general and concerns about managing work and family commitments. During the "young adult" stage, when children begin leaving home, families are usually less strained financially, and their concerns shift to reorganizing the household in response to their children's departure. Each stage of the family life cycle is different from those that came before and those that will follow.

These family life cycle changes are a regular part of the family's growth and development. Consequently, in order to understand the changing nature of family relationships throughout the family life cycle, we must take into account not only characteristics of the developing child or adolescent or young adult, but characteristics of the parents and of the family as a system at each stage of life.

A family life cycle perspective sees the family as a three or four generational system moving through time in a life cycle of distinct stages. During each stage the family is confronted with particular tasks to accomplish and challenges to face in order to prepare itself and its members for further growth and development. Viewing family life through a systems perspective can be a powerful tool for helping people understand what is happening in the life of their family and for creating strategies that promote individual and family faith growth and sharing.

Starting with the new couple, the following brief paragraphs describe the tasks faced by families at each stage of development. While no single development theory can explain all the factors that contribute to individual and family growth, such theories do provide windows through which we can gain a better understanding of how families change and grow. They help us understand what is happening in the life of the individual and in the life of the family as a whole.[2]

NEW COUPLE

Marriage joins not just two individuals, but two families together in a new relationship. It presents the new couple with a series of new challenges, including:

- defining and learning the role of husband and wife;
- establishing new relationships as a couple with their families of origin and with their friends;
- developing a commitment to a new family, with its own rules, roles, responsibilities, values and traditions.

As they confront these challenges, the new couple often finds themselves reflecting on the influence of their family of origin to draw insights, values and traditions that they want to include in their new family. This reflection helps them to sort out emotionally what they will take along from the family of origin, what they will leave behind and what they will create for themselves.

FAMILIES WITH CHILDREN

With the birth of the first child, the couple embarks on a new life task—to accept new members into the family and to adjust the rules, roles, responsibilities and relationships of their family to include the needs of the youngest members. The challenge for families with children involves:

- developing parenting roles and skills;
- negotiating and joining in childrearing, financial and household tasks;
- realigning relationships with extended family to include grandparenting roles;
- sharing socialization with the outside world;

■ developing new patterns of family communication, traditions, celebrations.

FAMILIES WITH ADOLESCENTS

Adolescence ushers in a new era in family life brought on by new adolescent life tasks and the changing role of the parents in relationship to their adolescent children. The changes of adolescence—puberty, new ways of thinking, wider sphere of social activity and relationships, greater autonomy—present the family as a whole with a new set of challenges. In fact, it would be fair to say that the whole family experiences adolescence. The challenge for families with adolescents involves:

■ allowing for the increasing independence of adolescents, while maintaining enough structure to foster continued family development;

■ reflection by adult members on their personal, marital and career life issues;

■ adjusting patterns of family communication, traditions, celebrations;

■ and for some families beginning the shift toward joint caring for the older generation.

The task for most families with adolescents—and it is by no means an easy one—is to maintain *emotional* involvement, in the form of concern and caring, while gradually moving toward a relationship characterized by greater *behavioral* autonomy.

FAMILIES WITH YOUNG ADULTS

The most significant aspect of this stage of life is that it is marked by the greatest number of exits and entries of family members. The stage begins with the launching of grown children into schooling, careers and homes of their own, and proceeds with the entry of their spouses and children. The challenge for families with young adults involves:

- regrouping as a family as each young adult moves out from the family;

- changes in the marital relationship now that parenting responsibilities are no longer required;

- development of adult-to-adult relationships between grown children and their parents;

- realigning relationships to include in-laws and grand-children;

- caring for the older generation and dealing with disabilities and death.

This stage of family life also presents unique challenges to the young adult, for example:

- accepting emotional and financial responsibility for oneself;

- formulating personal life goals;

- developing intimate peer relationships;

- establishing oneself in the world of work.

FAMILIES IN LATER LIFE

Among the tasks of families in later life is the adjustment to retirement, which not only may create the obvious vacuum for the retiring person, but may put a special strain on the marriage. Financial insecurity and dependence are also special difficulties, especially for family members who value managing for themselves. And while loss of friends and relatives is a particular difficulty at this phase, the loss of a spouse is the most difficult adjustment, with its problems of reorganizing one's entire life alone after many years as a couple and of having fewer relationships to help replace the loss. Grandparenthood can, however, offer a new lease on life and opportunities for special close relationships without the responsibilities of parenthood.

In this book we will describe many of the major characteristics and concerns of the older adolescent, as well as those of parents and the family as a whole. These explanations will help you to understand the changing nature of family relationships during adolescence and to offer practical suggestions for parenting and faith growth in families with teenagers.

HOW FAMILIES GROW IN FAITH

The Christian vision of family life speaks about the family as a community of life and love. It proclaims that family life is sacred and that family activities are holy, that God's love is revealed and communicated in new ways each and every day through Christian families. This Christian vision of family life calls families to a unique identity and mission. This means that the Christian family has several important responsibilities as it seeks to grow in faith:

- *Families form a loving community.*
  Families work to build a community based on love, compassion, respect, forgiveness and service to others. In families, people learn how to give and receive love and how to contribute to the good of other family members. In families, people open themselves to experiencing God's love through their dealings with one another, through the ethnic and cultural values and traditions that are part of family life and through the events of family life.

- *Families serve life by bearing and educating children.*
  Families serve life by bringing children into the world, by handing on Catholic Christian values and traditions and by developing the potential of each member at every age. As parents and all family members share their values with one another, they grow toward moral and spiritual maturity.

- *Families participate in building a caring and just society.*
  Families participate in building a caring and just society.

The gospel values of service, compassion and justice are first learned and practiced in families. In Christian families people learn how to reach out beyond the home to serve those in need and to work for justice for all God's people. How family members learn to relate to each other with respect, love, caring, fidelity, honesty and commitment becomes their way of relating to others in the world.

■ *Families share in the life and mission of the Church.*
Families share in the life and mission of the Church when the gospel vision and values are communicated and applied in daily life, when faith is celebrated through family rituals or through participation in the sacramental life of the church, when people gather as a family or parish community to pray, when people reach out, in Jesus' name, in loving service to others.

These responsibilities may sound overwhelming and unrealistic given all your other responsibilities as parents. In this book we will use these four responsibilities to develop practical ideas that you can use to share faith and promote individual and family faith growth. We will organize our ideas around six time-honored ways of sharing faith: (1) sharing the Catholic faith story, (2) celebrating faith through rituals, (3) praying together, (4) enriching family relationships, (5) responding to those in need through actions of justice and service, and (6) relating to the wider community.

Sharing the Catholic faith story happens when parents share stories from the Scriptures with their children, when families discuss the implications and applications of Christian faith for daily living, when a moral dilemma is encountered and the family turns to the resources of the Catholic faith for guidance, when parents discuss the religious questions their adolescents ask. The family's sharing is complemented by participation of children, parents and/or the entire family in the catechetical program of the parish community.

Celebrating faith through rituals happens when the family celebrates the liturgical year, such as Advent and

Christmas, Lent and Easter; celebrates the civic calendar, like Martin Luther King, Jr. Day and Earth Day; celebrates milestones or rites of passages, such as birthdays, anniversaries, graduations, special recognitions; celebrates ethnic traditions which have been passed down through the generations; celebrates the rituals of daily life, like meal prayer and forgiveness. These celebrations provide the foundations for a family ritual life in which God is discovered and celebrated through the day, week, month and year. The family's ritual life is complemented by participation in the ritual life of the parish community with its weekly celebration of the Eucharist; regular sacramental celebrations, such as Reconciliation and Anointing of the Sick; and liturgical year celebrations.

Praying together as a family is a reality when families incorporate prayer into the daily living through meal and bed times, times of thanksgiving and of crisis; when parents teach basic prayers and pray with their children. The family's prayer life is complemented by participation in the communal prayer life of the parish community, especially through liturgical year celebrations.

Enriching family relationships occurs when the family spends both quality and quantity time together; participates in family activities; works at developing healthy communication patterns which cultivate appreciation, respect and support for each other; negotiates and resolves problems and differences in positive and constructive ways. Enriching family relationships also involves the parents in developing their marriage relationship or a single parent developing intimate, supportive relationships in his or her life.

Performing acts of justice and service takes place when the family recognizes the needs of others in our communities and in our world and seeks to respond. Families act through stewardship and care for the earth; through direct service to others, the homeless and the hungry; through study of social issues; through developing a family lifestyle based on equality, nonviolence, respect for human dignity, respect for the earth. The family's service involvement is strengthened when it is done together with other families in the parish community.

Relating as a family to the wider community happens when families join together in family support groups or family clusters for sharing, activities and encouragement; when families learn about the broader church and world, especially the cultural heritages of others in the community or the world; when families organize to address common concerns facing them in the community, like quality education or safe neighborhoods.

This is quite a challenge for the family! Don't be overwhelmed. What is essential is that you identify how you already share faith using these six ways and try new approaches that will enrich your family life. In this book we have included ideas to support your current efforts and to encourage you to try new ways to share faith. Adapt and revise these ideas so that they work for you.

Remember that the family shares responsibility with the parish community for promoting faith growth in each of these six ways. A careful look at the six ways will reveal the basic functions of the parish community, e.g., religious education, sacraments and worship, serving the needs of others. The parish and family approach each of these six ways of sharing faith differently. The parish community needs to support and encourage the efforts of families to share faith. Families need to be involved in the life of the parish community so that their family efforts can be connected to the larger community of faith. Don't be afraid to challenge your parish community and its leaders to support families and to offer programs and services for families that will promote the family's growth in faith.

GROWING TOWARD MATURITY IN FAITH

What do we hope will happen in the lives of family members—parents and children alike—if we strengthen our efforts at sharing faith? It is our hope that family members will

discover meaning and purpose for their lives in a life-trans-
forming relationship with a loving God in Jesus Christ and a
consistent devotion to serving others as Jesus did.

Our growth as Catholic Christians is never complete. It
is a life-long journey towards greater maturity in faith. While
no complete description of this journey is possible, we hope
and pray that you and your family will grow toward a living
faith characterized by the following elements:

- trusting in God's saving grace and firmly believing in
  the humanity and divinity of Jesus Christ;

- experiencing a sense of personal well-being, security
  and peace;

- integrating faith and life—seeing work, family, social
  relationships and political choices as part of your religious life;

- seeking spiritual growth through Scripture, study,
  reflection, prayer and discussion with others;

- seeking to be part of a Catholic community of believers
  in which people give witness to their faith, support and
  nourish one another, serve the needs of each other and
  the community, and worship together;

- developing a deeper understanding of the Catholic
  Christian tradition and its applicability to life in
  today's complex society;

- holding life-affirming gospel values, including respect
  for human dignity, commitment to uphold human
  rights, equality (especially racial and gender), stewardship, care and compassion and a personal sense of
  responsibility for the welfare of others;

- advocating for social and global change to bring about
  greater social justice and peace;

- serving humanity, consistently and passionately,
  through acts of love and justice.

Families provide a natural context for nurturing God's gift of faith. As families and individuals grow together in faith, life is enriched and the gospel vision brought closer to reality. Faith and family are a natural duo. May this volume be one small step toward helping you grow together more effectively.

End Notes

[1] These points about effective parenting were summarized from *Back to the Family* by Ray Guarendi (New York: Villard Books, 1990).

[2] The family life cycle perspective described below was adapted from "The Family Life Cycle," by Betty Carter and Monica McGoldrick in *Growing in Faith: A Catholic Family Sourcebook,* ed. John Roberto (New Rochelle: Don Bosco Multimedia, 1990.)

2

UNDERSTANDING FAMILIES WITH OLDER ADOLESCENTS

It was a special night. Audrey's new boss was coming for dinner and two of our adolescents were being unusually helpful in the kitchen. Her new position was, in their words, "a big deal," so they were trying to be supportive, and Audrey was enjoying one of those times when having teenagers was rewarding. They seemed genuinely interested in her concerns and she felt as if she had two friends in the kitchen. Just then, though, the phone rang. Instantly, one of our daughters dropped the potato peeler, leapt in front of Audrey and knocked a dish off the counter as she flew to the phone, leaving in her jet stream a hasty, "Oops! Sorry, Mom. I think it's Jim." That was the last Audrey saw of her until we called her for dinner. The meal was enjoyable, but just before dessert our son announced that he had forgotten to tell us that he had to be driven to basketball practice in 15 minutes. His older sister said, "It's OK, Mom and Dad. I'll drive him. Just enjoy your dessert!" We felt another moment of pride that we enjoyed doubly as we realized how thoughtful it must look to our guest. As dessert was finished and we were about to enjoy a cup of coffee, the phone rang again. This time it was for us. It was the police. They had our 16-year-old generous and thoughtful driver at the station for speeding and driving without her license. Our short-lived pride quickly turned to embarrassment as we rescued her from the station after explaining the situation to Audrey's new boss. How awful! From the kitchen to the police station, from pride to embarrassment, all in a couple of hours. Welcome to the world of parenting adolescents.

A family goes through many experiences like this as it tackles the ups and downs of life with adolescents. Our unforgettable dinner often comes to mind when I think about families with teenagers. Very often a new job for a parent is part of this cycle as is the young person's swing from concern for the parents to complete abandonment should the right phone call come. Life with teenagers can be unpredictable and uncontrollable, frustrating and rewarding—but never dull!

The family with teenage children (ranging from 13-to 20-years old) can be facing some of the most challenging times in the family's growth. There is a very interesting research that shows the frustration many parents feel as they work their way through their children's adolescent years. For the first three stages (marriage through preschoolers) more than 50 percent of the couples studied reported that their present stage was "very satisfying." Satisfaction waned for the next three stages (school-age children until the first child leaves home) with only ten percent of the couples reporting their current stage as "very satisfying."

It makes sense. Some parents are hitting their "mid-life crisis" at the same time their adolescents are struggling to develop their own personalities. Some parents are dealing with an adolescent after a divorce, complicated by having to deal with visits from and discuss sensitive issues with the absent parent. Some parents are finding grey hairs while their teens are struggling with puberty. Some parents, having given birth to their child during their own teenage years, are tackling young adult issues themselves as their child reaches adolescence. Some parents are trying to blend two families, and the normal self-centeredness of the adolescent makes it all the more difficult. In other words, it's pretty normal to find that raising teen children is difficult and frustrating. It can be a little easier and more satisfying, though, if you prepare for the special tasks and needs of families with adolescents and acknowledge that it may be hard, and that you are not alone in feeling that way!

Let's take an in-depth look at families with adolescents. We will look at the relationship between the parents and the adolescents and the relationship between the parents, individually and as a couple.

RELATIONSHIP BETWEEN PARENTS AND ADOLESCENTS

The parent-teen relationship will challenge everyone involved to grow, or it will begin to slowly die. Either way, it involves a little pain. We would like to describe some of the issues unique to families with adolescents and share with you some ideas on how individuals and families can cope *and* facilitate growth.

Teen Independence... "I can do it myself."

This is a phrase parents of adolescents often hear. But more and more often than ever before, they really can do it themselves. As we continue to strive toward building a strong and healthy relationship with our adolescents, we must realize that our young people are becoming more and more independent. We watch with pride and apprehension as they insist, "I can do it myself," and try to keep loosening the reins by appropriate amounts as each new challenge arrives. How tightly should we hold on as dating becomes serious? How much can we loosen the reins when they start their first job? Unfortunately, there are no easy answers or fool-proof guidelines. If we don't allow more and more independence, how can we expect to see a mature and self-sufficient adult emerge?

Our teens are full of contradictions, though, and don't know themselves, yet, how much independence they can handle. They drive our car but don't welcome any advice on handling it, until they phone for help with a flat tire or are trapped at the police station in need of a parent's signature. They pick out their own clothes, and much to the chagrin of many parents, choose their own individualistic hairstyle. (How many parent-teen relationships have been damaged by "discussions" over a new hair style?) Our young people will proudly find a job but then depend on us for transportation. Each episode is only a stepping stone on their journey to independence. If we strive for a successful journey, we will have to let them step on some of the slippery stepping stones and even stand by now and then and watch them "fall off." We become less and less captains of their journey and more and more loving companions.

Parental Flexibility..."But, dad, this is different."

Sometimes it seems to us that our children think that every situation is "different." "Are they just being manipulative or should we bend this time?" we constantly ask ourselves. Parents in a family with adolescents who want to maintain a strong relationship with their offspring will need to learn to be flexible. Household rules, such as curfews, can become more effective when they become more flexible. Often it helps to set them according to the particular event or situation, rather than a mandatory and inflexible time. Maybe as a parent you like to call it a night at midnight and it would be easier for you if your adolescent was home, but that can't always work. For instance, we know a teen whose curfew is rigidly set at 11:30 PM. After working at a local fast food restaurant until 9:00 PM, the only weekend movies he could attend were at 9:30 or 9:45. That young person walked out on the climax of several films in order to get home by the 11:30 deadline, and his resentment towards parents grew every time. Even though he lived up to the curfew, his relationship with his parents suffered; a little flexibility on their part would have paid wonderful dividends. The rigid tree breaks in the storm; the tree that sways and bends with the wind survives and flourishes.

Balancing consistency and flexibility in household rules and expectations can be particularly challenging in blended families or in situations where young people move regularly between the homes of separated or divorced parents. Whatever the family structure, mutual respect, support and communication are needed between all parents united in the task of parenting an adolescent.

While flexibility is important, it is also essential that when you bend the rules, you explain why. Perhaps R-rated movies are not common fare on your VCR, but your adolescents have many opportunities to see them elsewhere. Can we really protect them from the world and its crummy movies, or are we better off helping them to learn by critically analyzing them? To teach these skills, we need to talk—and listen—a lot. Merely condemning an R-rated movie is not as effective as discussing the values portrayed in the film, and the fact that a movie has box office appeal doesn't mean that it's a "good" movie. This not only teaches teens to think critically but builds a stronger parent-teen relationship. The family boundaries then become a guide for belief and behavior and not a prison to hold them in.

Permeable Family Boundaries..."But, mom, this is the '90s. It's not the same as when you were a kid."

It certainly isn't the same. It's a difficult world, an electronic age with easy access to drugs and many depressed people. It's a beautiful world, too, an age where you can instantly communicate with loved ones around the world; an age with medicines that cure diseases that our ancestors died from; an age full of people willing to serve others in hundreds of volunteer corps around the world. Either way, we are parenting in a world much different than the one we grew up in. "Family" is a much more encompassing word and the boundaries are much less rigid. In families with adolescents, the relationship between the parents and the young people will be stronger if the family boundaries are more permeable. Our young people are striving to belong as well as differentiate themselves (from family and friends) as unique individuals. This can only be done if they can move in and out of the family boundaries often. And move back and forth, they do. For many young people from single parent or blended families, this movement is a regular part of life. The move back and forth between different homes and lifestyles can be an occasion for tension or for growth depending on how it is handled by the adults involved.

Are these family boundaries the same for all the adolescents in a family? Ideally, perhaps, but in our family, what was true for our older children is not necessarily true for our younger ones. The family size and dynamics are quite different for our youngest than they were for our oldest. If our family life is separated from the outside world by a large and heavy door secured with many locks and bolts, our young people may be discouraged by the effort it takes to open the door every time they want to experience the outside world. They may choose, instead, to seldom venture out or stay out and seldom venture home. If our family life is, however, on one side of a revolving door, our adolescents will be freer to come and go, and our relationship with them will be enhanced—even energized by those crazy, but memorable times we've all had as our children come and go, and enrich our lives with the experiences they have with their friends, teachers, coaches and other family members.

Parental Authority...“You can’t make me. You parents don’t know everything.”

Our young people remind us of this often. In a family with adolescents, we, the parents, are no longer the complete authority in the lives of our children that we were in their younger days. As our young people develop their lives separate from ours, they will seek out other authorities in their quest. Adolescents are often found refusing your parental advice only to accept it wholeheartedly from a coach, teacher or other significant adult. As our adolescents internalize and make their own decisions about what is important and what isn’t in their lives, we can help them by communicating and discussing things with them not as authoritative parents, but as caring adults, who have confidence in their ability to manage their own lives. Regardless of family structure, parents need to agree on basic guidelines and support one another on major issues. The dynamics will differ from family to family, but the goal remains the same—to help young people take increased personal responsibility for their own lives and decisions. As one of our children told us when she was in high school, “I know what you think about premarital sex, but I don’t necessarily have to think the same thing.” It was with the mixed emotions of pride in her growth; fear of the scary possibilities; and dependence on prayers to God for her happiness, that I answered, “I know, honey. I trust you’ll figure it out for yourself. I just love you and I want you to be happy. And I worry about the choices that will endanger that happiness.” No longer being the complete authority in your adolescent’s life is scary, but it is also freeing.

Influence of the Adolescent’s Friends...“But my friend said...”

What friends say carries a lot of weight. The world of adolescents is a world of friendships, some healthy and some destructive. Either way, friends are most important and highly influential. A wise parent learns early to pay attention to friends and their lifestyles. As a parent of an adolescent, you soon realize that the friends of your teenager have a major influence upon the choices and lifestyle of your off-spring. Your relationship with your teen will grow or deteriorate in direct proportion to how you receive their friends. This may seem like a strong statement, but it has definitely been part of our experience. Accepting your teenager's friends is an important part of living through this stage. We must be careful to accept their friends even if their behavior leads to some intense discussion and compromise. Our acceptance can be a lesson in Christian love and a model for our young people. When we accept the person without unquestioningly affirming all of their behaviors, we set a strong example.

Knowing your adolescent's friends will tell you a lot about your son or daughter. Getting to know them will help the bond between you. And even though adolescents often resist their parents attempts to meet their friends, they are always pleased when their friends like their mom or dad. Communicating with the parents of your teen's friends is also a plus.

Fluctuation between Independence and Dependence..."I can't wait to get my driver's license."

Families with adolescents experience a lot of fluctuation. Teens may move from feeling independent and confident to dependent and insecure several times a day! There is no more confident and independent feeling teenager than the one who steps out of the motor vehicle office with the first driver's license still warm from the laminating machine. The excitement gives way to reality rather quickly when the money for gas becomes an issue or the first traffic ticket appears with their name on it. Making money and having a job mean a lot to independent teenagers, but they don't expect to spend their earnings on school fees and dental bills. Teens who will adamantly let you know that they have a right to go without a winter jacket, if they choose, will also expect you to take them to the doctor and pick up the prescription for bronchitis medication when they get sick.

The adolescent years are the years our young people can "test out" their independence, knowing they have you to fall back on. They can claim independence when it suits them and retreat to dependence when life is too hard. Wise parents increase their adolescents' independence and diminish the dependence gradually as the years pass. This gradual process helps to prepare and nurture our offspring for when they will be on their own and we'll all be a family of interdependent adults.

Relationship with Extended Family Members..."You parents don't understand as well as Aunt Beth does."

The relationship between a parent and an adolescent often takes on a new dimension as the teen reaches out and forms independent relationships with grandparents, aunts, uncles and others. In single parent and step families, relationships may blossom in new ways with the non-custodial parent or step parent. It can be hard for a parent to see how close their son or daughter may become to another adult, and you may feel a twinge of jealousy. But these independent relationships with others only broaden the young person's social skills, human resources and ability to love, and your relationship can only benefit from them. This stage demands more open and honest sharing to shape a new relationship based on less control and more discussion. Although it is often a struggle, the strength of the parent-teen relationship has a lot to do with the overall "health" of the family.

RELATIONSHIPS AND ISSUES IN THE LIVES OF THE PARENTS

With all of the emotional demands of their adolescents, parents need to remember that their relationship with each other needs continual nurturing, too.

The Parents' Relationship as a Couple

For some families, the relationship between husband and wife is challenged as they must simultaneously work to parent their adolescent, face their own mid-life issues and often care for their aging parents. Come and peek in on one of our Friday nights.

> It was a typical weekend night at our house with the phone ringing off the hook as our adolescent children made plans for their "night out." Audrey and I had already planned to see a movie together; it had been weeks since we had a "date." As Audrey finished the dinner preparations, she checked the time—5:20 PM—which meant there was still time to eat together, clean up, and get to the theater by 7:15 PM. Her thoughts were interrupted by the phone, followed by a teen voice shouting, "Mom, Grandma's on the phone." Audrey picked up the receiver and heard her mother's upset voice. "My car won't start and I have to get up to the hospital to feed your dad his dinner," she said. "Can you take me?" Her mom seemed so urgent, so alone and so needy, how could she say, "No"? After all, since her father's recent heart attack her mom had been at the hospital every day and only a few time had she asked for assistance. Realizing that hospital visiting hours ended at 8:00 PM and that we could still see the 9:20 movie, Audrey told her she would take her to the hospital.
>
> As dinner was put on the table, Audrey began to explain the situation to me when she was interrupted by our 14-year-old daughter who announced, "Dad, I know you said you and Mom were going to a 7:15 movie so driving me to Jenny's birthday party at 7:30 was out. I got a ride with Linda. Her mom will take us to the party so all you'll have to do is pick us up at 11:00. I told her that would be okay since your early movie will be out by then." In a matter of only minutes, our "date" was all but erased. Audrey was disappointed with me for promising to

drive our daughter without discussing it, and I was irritated with Audrey for presuming we could switch our movie time without asking. Our date turned into a hurried hour together between a visit to the hospital and chauffeuring our freshman. It was okay, but much less fulfilling than the evening together we had been looking forward to. It really made us feel like our lives and our relationship were only sandwiched in between the lives of our adolescents and the lives of our parents.

The "sandwich generation" is an expression we've experienced and come to understand intimately. As the months rolled by and a fatal heart attack claimed the life of Audrey's father, we experienced lots of challenges as we helped care for her mom until her death. We dealt with the financial and emotional strains and still, somehow, had to meet our needs and those of our adolescents. It meant keeping family communication open, both with each other and with our teenagers so they could understand our motives and choices and live comfortably with all that was happening. Regardless of the length of the marriage or the current structure of the family unit, parents need to make time to respond to their personal and couple needs.

New Relationships for a Single Parent

For families headed by a single parent, life with adolescents presents other challenges. For example, both the parent and teen may be dating and seeking new identities simultaneously. This can create a lot of "nitty gritty" complications. Who gets the bathroom first when there is only one? Who gets the only family car? How does a parent supervise a teen's curfew if the parent is out also? What about money for dating and use of the phone? And how do you explain it all to grandma?

For single parents, any new relationship (whether romantic or simply a new friend) means dealing with a lot of complex issues at once: letting go of and mourning their previous relationships severed by death or divorce; nervousness about meeting new people; the scrutiny of their new friends by their teenage offspring; unsolicited advice from extended family members; and sometimes interference from ex-spouses. The parent is challenged to deal with tough issues and still maintain a balance in meeting their needs and the needs of their adolescents. Once again, honest communication is vital.

Renegotiation of Family Roles

By the time children are adolescents, a family has a history with family patterns all its own, some positive and some destructive. In a two-parent home, sometimes the husband and wife have devoted themselves so diligently to careers and parenting that they have neglected to nurture their own relationship. The marriage relationship can just be taken for granted or perhaps even seen as "getting boring." Into this experience enters the adolescent who is primarily interested in himself and very good at "playing one parent against the other." Sandwiched between aging parents and demanding adolescents, where does a couple find time for their own personal needs and the very real needs of their relationship as a couple?

One of the ways we have tried to nurture our relationship is to "date" regularly. The goal is admirable and, as discussed, we aimed for Friday nights, only to find that high school sports and chauffeuring our adolescents were only a few of the roadblocks. We then decided to switch to Sunday mornings, a time our adolescents rarely interrupt since they seldom get up much before noon. Struggling to hold onto a regular time and stay within our budget, we have had many dates just sitting on a bench in a local park talking and sharing our frustrations and our dreams.

We sometimes find it difficult parenting adolescents with two parents, but a single parent faces all of the same tough issues without that support. This is often combined with the difficulties of sharing the adolescents with an absent parent. There is often a legitimate need for a single parent to renegotiate with their adolescent children the amount of time allotted for parenting and for personal issues. Another complication some families face is that blending two families requires all sorts of renegotiation among family members to balance the needs of parents and offspring.

Career Issues

An issue that directly affects the family with adolescents is the career choices that the adults must make. Take, for example, a parent who has been working at the same job for the last fifteen to twenty years and is beginning to realize that there is no room for advancement. They must decide whether to accept that reality or try to make a job or career change with all of the uncertainties that entails, such as loss of retirement and health benefits. The parent is torn between seeking more job satisfaction and the responsibility of financially providing for the family.

Different difficulties are faced by the parent who is now, because of death or divorce, the sole provider for the family. This financial uncertainty and stress can directly affect relationships in the family. In a blended family, the two adults who have been raising separate families may need to make a job or career move or choose to relocate. To complicate matters even more, a family with adolescents often finds the parent handling the stress of job or career choices at the same time the adolescent is adjusting to having a first part-time job. Trying to juggle the use of the car and family vacation time around yet another schedule can create problems unless everyone is communicating clearly.

When both parents are working, there are many decisions to be made. Who leaves work early when an adolescent has to be taken to traffic court? Which parent is responsible for chauffeuring adolescents home from late night school activities when both are tired and have to go to work the next morning? Who is responsible when the demands of jobs or careers interfere with their relationship? How are the daily family chores negotiated or shared with both parents working and adolescents skilled in avoiding such mundane tasks as dishes or laundry?

All of these situations force parents to balance their job and career choices between financial support and emotional support of their offspring; it is not an easy task and, unfortunately, rarely presents clear-cut choices.

Personal Issues

Personal issues such as health, stress and personal friendships also challenge parents. For some, mid-life has added pounds and new aches and pains. For others, finding time to exercise seems impossible. And just keeping on top of a teen's social life robs parents of sleep. Parents of adolescents, who need all of their strength all the time, should be especially careful to watch their diets, get regular check-ups and watch their smoking and drinking. Raising adolescents can be stressful!

Indeed, as parents we face stress on many levels: dealing with our job or career issues and changes; living through adolescent moods and demands; managing our own relationship; building new relationships after a death or divorce, or blending two families into a new family after a marriage; and, for some of us, meeting the needs of aging parents. Being able to creatively handle stress and having the support of good friends can make the years with your adolescent much easier.

The personal friendships that have been such an important part of our life seem harder to manage. Where does time with friends fit in the schedule already strained to include all of the things we need to fit into a day? For years we enjoyed the support of a very special group of friends in our parish. We met faithfully one Friday night a month to share family stories, brainstorm solutions to family problems (from toddler toilet training to junior high academics to couple communication) and even pray together. We shared our problems, recipes, tears, jokes, cars, birthdays and wedding anniversaries, and even our children since we often babysat for each other.

These times were very special and initially were not too difficult to arrange. We just agreed to meet at 8:30 PM: time enough to get infants to bed and prepare the others for the babysitter. It was only as our children became adolescents that these Friday nights became a problem. The first few times we missed we were cheering on our children at ball games. Other times we missed because our mom was recuperating from a severe heart attack and couldn't be left alone. A few times we missed because our jobs demanded our presence at a special meeting or event; then we began missing regularly to chauffeur our adolescents or to be home when a daughter wanted to entertain a boyfriend. We felt our presence at home on Friday nights deterred problems, such as unsupervised parties. Being home also gives us the opportunity to meet our teenagers' friends. The Friday nights we have missed our adult group in order to make pizza for a group of teens or just "be around" have paid great dividends in increased communication with our adolescents and in our knowledge of their friends. Even though we've seen our own friends less often, we look forward to re-establishing those regular bonds when our adolescents become young adults.

Economic Issues

Parents also face unique economic issues. Besides the strain of the usual bills, there is often the issue of transportation for the adolescent, the question of college or technical school, expenses for care of older parents and sometimes even impending wedding expenses. While teenagers' part-time jobs helps them learn a lot about working, responsibility, time management and self-discipline, it often means an added transportation need. Auto insurance alone can put quite a strain on the budget. As parents of young children we were always amazed at how much of our family budget went to pay pediatricians and baby-sitters. Now that we've added cars, teenage auto insurance and school tuitions, our pediatrician bills seem minor.

Parents of adolescents often find their salaries are unable to meet their increased financial responsibilities. Some parents must get a second part-time job or search for a better paying job. Money becomes a tough issue for the family with adolescents, especially when coupled with the intense emotion that surrounds the use of the car or the price of a prom dress. We are also trying to teach our adolescent children about

Christian values and how they affect our lifestyle choices. We have had many "discussions" about family finances, some quite emotional and explosive, some successful and effective.

Financial issues can be especially challenging in single parent and blended families where funds are limited and/or complicated by issues of what's mine, yours and ours. Whether financial resources in blended families are carefully differentiated, or pooled together and distributed according to need instead of blood ties, family members need to sit down, talk through the emotions and issues related to how money is spent and agree on how financial matters will be handled.

CONCLUSION: FAMILIES WITH ADOLESCENTS

It is very important to remember that the changes in adolescents and in their parents affects the entire system of relationships in the family. The concerns and issues characteristic of families at adolescence arise not just because of the changing needs and concerns of the young person but also because of changes in the parents and because of changes in the needs and functions of the family as a unit. Consequently, in order to understand the changing nature of family relationships during the adolescent years, we must take into account not only characteristics of the developing young person but characteristics of the parents and of families at this stage as well.

As we have seen, adolescence ushers in a new era in family life brought on by new adolescent life tasks and the changing role of the parents in relationship to their adolescent children. The changes of adolescence—puberty, new ways of thinking, wider sphere of social activity and relationships, greater autonomy—present the family as a whole with a new set of challenges. In fact, it would be fair to say that the whole family experiences adolescence.

The challenge for families with adolescents involves:

- allowing for the increasing independence of adolescents, while maintaining enough structure to foster continued family development;

- reflecting by adult members on their personal, marital and career life issues;

- adjusting patterns of family communication, traditions, celebrations;

- and for some families, beginning the shift toward joint caring for the older generation.

These changes in the family system during adolescence bring about periods of disequilibrium or imbalance—times when an individual member has changed but the system has not yet fully adapted by altering relationships. A healthy family system will adapt to this new stage in the family life cycle—bringing about balance or equilibrium. These changes in family relationships occur gradually, in a somewhat disorganized fashion, as individuals try on new roles and experiment with new ways of relating to each other.

The task for most families with adolescents—and it is by no means an easy one—is to maintain *emotional* involvement, in the form of concern and caring, while gradually moving toward a relationship characterized by greater *behavioral* autonomy.

A family with adolescents is definitely a family tackling tough issues. Because it is often a struggle, the parent is often tempted to focus on a destination—the end of the adolescent stage. Yet there is much to be said for the journey as well. Any parent of adolescents has already nurtured another human being for more than a decade. We believe that from the seeds of both our failures and successes, God will harvest much. At no other time in our lives have we been more challenged to re-think, to listen with every ounce of our being, to look inward as well as outward, to laugh, to reclaim or revise our own values, to love unconditionally, to forgive, to go one more mile when we didn't think we had it in us, to persevere and especially to grow. At no other time in our lives have we felt the intense joy that the journey has afforded.

When our oldest was married, we spent a whole afternoon the week before her wedding just reminiscing, letting go, hugging to hold on, crying, laughing and joyfully looking forward to the future. We rejoiced in our own relationship as she chose to wear her mother's 26-year-old wedding gown because she felt it "represented a strong bond." And we also rejoiced in our relationship with the Church as we celebrated a meaningful liturgy and witnessed our daughter's new married life begin.

It's not just the destination that matters. It's also the way we make the journey.

3

PARENTING SKILLS
FOR FAITH GROWTH

What are the parenting skills we need now that we are living in a house full of teenagers? What are the skills that make a difference in nurturing and guiding adolescents to share our Catholic faith? Here are some of the specific parenting techniques that helped us as we have tried to share faith with our young people.

COMMUNICATION

First, and most important, is communication. We must talk "with" adolescents, not to them. Talking "with" them can be risky because your own ideas will be challenged and maybe even re-shaped, but one of the rewards of this stage is how exciting and energizing it is to see the special people our children are becoming. When dealing with teenagers, we need to be able to articulate our faith beliefs in non-judgmental ways without preaching. For instance, it's one thing to say, "I feel so grateful to God for all I've been given that I want to go Mass and say 'Thank you.'" It's another thing to discuss Sunday Mass attendance by saying, "As long as you live in my house, you will go to Mass!"

We need to communicate our faith in God through everyday conversations just as naturally as we communicate about our other relationships and activities. Letting our young people know that our conversations with God are as frequent and as real as our conversations with others is a real plus.

Sometimes our attempts to communicate with our teenagers work and sometimes they don't. Keeping communications channels open can be a real challenge in cases where a young person splits his or her time between two homes. It is likewise an ongoing challenge in blended families where different approaches to discipline come into play or where the relationships between young people and their step parents are still being worked out.

There are many good books and articles about improving communication skills, and we constantly try to work on ours. Active listening is a term that proposes a concentrated effort to hear not only a person's words but the feelings between the lines. We then re-phrase and reflect back to the speaker not only what they said but how they're feeling. It teaches the skill of actively listening, checking out the message we think we hear by reflecting it back and then proceeding after clarification.

In addition to improving our communication skills, we have found three things to be vital when working with our adolescents: timing, humor and listening. Whenever possible, we have found it helpful to discuss things when the emotional climate was favorable and our teens were ready. Unfortunately, that rarely seemed to be at a time that was good for us. (It doesn't seem fair: if you try to ask your teenager a question in the middle of their nightly "phone hour" with that "special" person, you'll be ignored. But try to ignore their question when you're on the phone and they need something!)

The most productive discussions on dating, for instance, have come late at night after our teen's arrival home after a date, when we "just happened" to be up but were ready to go to sleep. The best conversations about their academic struggles seem to come right after school when they are complaining about a test grade and need a sympathetic ear, even if you are trying to concentrate on a new recipe you are cooking. No matter: when they are ready to talk you are more likely to be guaranteed success as long as you can effectively mentally and emotionally set other things aside. If you can't, it helps to say something like, "You are important to me and I really want our conversation to get my full attention, but right now I'm distracted by this cooking I have to do. Can we talk right after dinner?" For us it's important to set a specific time, since "later" doesn't always happen. Either way, timing is important for successful conversations.

Second, we have found the use of humor invaluable to loosen tension. Not that every serious conversation should become a joke, for that can deteriorate to sarcasm and hurt feelings, but genuine attempts to smile together are helpful. For instance, once when Audrey took one of our daughters to the doctor, he sent them to a lab for her first blood test. The more anxious our daughter became, the more obnoxious she became. The longer they waited, the more condescending and negative she became. Audrey felt her anger rising, and thought perhaps a little humor might help. So when our daughter asked sarcastically, "Which arm will they put the needle in, or don't you know?," with a smile Audrey answered, "Well, it depends. First we adults get together and decide which one will hurt most. Then, of course, we choose that one." Our teen grinned and said, "Seriously, Mom. Do they pick a certain arm?" Instantly her tone changed and communication improved. Audrey avoided becoming angry and our teen realized how nervous she was.

Our children have also found this approach helpful in reverse. One morning before school Audrey was in a crabby and unapproachable mood. Our 14-year-old tried to get beyond it, but then disappeared to her room. Later she shouted, "Bye," and left with her 16-year-old sister, who was going to drive her to school. All of a sudden she ran back in the house, saying, "Mom, I wanted to let you know you just flunked Mother's School. You forgot to tell us to wear our seat belts." She gave Audrey a quick peck on the cheek and ran back outside before she could respond. Audrey quickly recovered and ran out to the car, tapped on the window, and begged the girls for another chance to take "the Mother's School exam," and everyone laughed. It is amazing how that little bit of humor changed everyone's day!

When communicating with our adolescents we always try to listen more than we talk. We have so much we want to say and teach, that often we only half listen, just waiting for our chance to give our advice and share our wisdom. Our teens have lots to say too, though, and often we find that if we really listen to them, we end up re-shaping the "great" advice we were waiting to give. Our teens have painfully shared with us how everyone (teachers, coaches, bosses, etc.) tells them what to do, but only their friends truly listen. So we try not to make the same mistake. When communicating with our young people, we have found timing, humor and real listening to be essential.

BE ACCEPTING OF THEIR WAY

We will never forget the day we realized how much we judged our teens behavior from our own perspective. It was 3:00 (15 minutes after our 8th grade daughter had walked in the door from school), and she was already on the phone. We knew she could easily spend the next hour there, and it was becoming a pattern with which we were not happy. Later that afternoon Audrey decided to discuss the issue with her. Our daughter had explained how important the phone was to her when Audrey said, "I can't understand why you need to be on the phone all afternoon with friends you've talked to all day at school." Our daughter quickly answered, "That's just the point! I don't get to talk to them all day. We're in separate classes and we have to eat lunch in our homerooms, so even though I am at school all day we don't get to talk at all. It's frustrating." Things suddenly looked different, but until we listened we didn't realize it. We ended up compromising; she could spend the hour on the phone in the afternoon as long as she did her homework at another time.

Another time, we were concerned that we never saw our children pray; it always seemed the radio and the earphones were top priority. It turned out though, that their ways of praying just didn't look like it from our perspective. Our 14-year-old daughter shared a special cassette tape of modern songs she had made to pray with. She affectionately called it her "God tape" and explained, "Just think God, Mom and Dad, and sing along." We heard songs like, "You're the inspiration...You bring meaning to my life;" "Stand by me....I won't be afraid if only you'll stand by me;" and, "I just called to say 'I Love You.'" We prayed for the homeless singing Phil Collins' "Another Day in Paradise," and for our deceased parents with, "The Living Years." To this day we cherish our copy of our teenager's "God tape."

Incidents like this have taught us to be less quick to judge. We've learned first, to share our way as *one* way not *the* way. Second, we've learned to look at their way of doing things as not better or worse, but just different. Third, we've learned to share the "why" of the decisions and choices we make and seek the "why" of their ways. Through this process we have all grown, and we keep working to be more accepting, especially when our children's decisions differ from ours.

LETTING GO

Perhaps the hardest and most risky part of parenting adolescents is learning to let go. If you let go too early, your teens will be in trouble; if you hold on too tight, they rebel. The hard part is learning how much to let go—and when. For example, if we gave in to our 14-year-old's complaints about having to go to "boring Sunday Masses," I'm sure that would be the end of weekend liturgy. On the other hand, we cannot effectively force our 19-year-old college sophomore, away at school, to show up at Sunday Mass. It is a policy in our home that, starting when you are 16, half of all the money you make goes into the bank for college and future necessities. There are also some guidelines about sharing your money with those in need. We have little to say, though, about how money that is earned on a part-time job away at school is spent. Our younger teenagers have a specific curfew for each night out, arrived at individually after considering the event, who is driving and the teenager involved. Our seniors, though, set their own curfew, based on the experiences of the earlier three years. These are some of the ways we have tried to gradually increase our teenagers' responsibility for self-support step-by-step each year, so that when they are on their own, they are used to budgeting their time and money. When families divorce, it can be difficult to guarantee a united approach to helping a young person grow in his or her sense of responsibility. On the other hand, adapting to life in two homes or with two sets of parents can increase young people's adaptability and enhance their sense of personal responsibility for their actions.

How do you decide when to let go and when to hold on? First, make prayer a part of every decision. There is power in prayer and we call on that power often. Second, look to others who have gone before you. Share your concerns with other families, friends and relatives who you respect and admire. Some of our best parenting tips have come from other parents with children just a few years older than ours. The desire to share parenting issues and approaches with parents in similar situations has led to the establishment of support groups for separated, divorced and blended families. Check the availability of these and similar groups in your area. Third, learn about adolescent development. Reading about adolescent growth and parenting or attending a parenting class at your local church or school can be very helpful. These experiences also teach us that we are not alone and that a lot of what we are experiencing is quite normal.

Fourth, base your decision on how much freedom to allow in each situation on the teenager before you, their past record and your previous experiences. What is good for one son or daughter might not be for another. Fifth, try letting go in small steps until both you and your teenager are comfortable. Each small step taken successfully builds trust and makes the next step easier. And each small step that doesn't work is easier to re-take than giant moves in the wrong direction. Try one weekend with the teenager deciding the curfew. If it works well, try another. If it doesn't you don't have to undo your whole style of living since the rules applied to only one weekend. Sixth, plan on making lots of mistakes. The myth of the perfect parent is just that a myth. Even those with "A's" in Parenting School learned from mistakes. Our young people need the message that mistakes are a part of life and even the best of people make some, so just admit them and move on, taking with you the invaluable knowledge that results.

Letting go of our adolescent children is one of parenting's hardest tasks. But grown men and women all start out as teenage boys or girls. Watching our adolescents evolve into self-sufficient, happy, productive adults is sometimes painful, but the more skilled we become at letting go creatively, the more joy we can feel. If they make choices that are destructive, we need to remind ourselves that all of their choices are not our fault. As adults they will make choices with which we won't agree. Having spent a good portion of our lives trying to be loving parents, we must stop asking, "Where did I go wrong?" and start asking for the strength to accept.

CREATIVE DISCIPLINE

Living with adolescents and changing the style of discipline that was effective with fourth graders challenges the best of parents. It helps to start by distinguishing between the really important issues and lesser problems. A phrase that really summed it up for us was, "Don't major in the minors." If you're constantly arguing with your teenager about minor things (a clean room, bedtime or their hairstyle), you won't have much of a chance of being heard when it comes to the major ones (substance abuse, sexuality, religion, etc.). You might win a lot of battles and have a son or daughter with a clean room and a neat hairstyle, but you might also lose the war if he or she totally rebels.

Although the skills needed for creative discipline with adolescents are basically the same for all families, some families face special challenges. Single parents who carry the responsibility for discipline alone can find it difficult, at times, to balance the needs for supporting and providing structure for their children. In blended families, and especially new ones with "instant" teenage children, young people may reject discipline attempts by a new step parent. In any family, children may attempt to play off one parent against the other. While parents may not always agree on all issues, discipline is easiest when parents, family members and friends support one another in this crucial task.

Let's consider some of the principles of creative discipline. First, behavior has consequences. If we don't pay our electric bill, they shut off our lights; if we don't show up for work, we won't get paid. It's important to be sure to set policies and rules with clear consequences. For example, in our house if you violate curfew, you are grounded for a weekend. If you don't help with household chores, you can't use the car. Phone calls made after an agreed upon hour means the phone is off-limits for two days. With such policies in place, discipline is easier and teens are not subject to rash threats in parental fits of anger.

Second, to be effective, it is important to be sure that the consequences have some connection to the behavior. So, missing Mass results in going to church another time, for instance. This effort to match actions and consequences teaches rather than punishes.

What happens, though, when the behavior has not been discussed and consequences are not clear? Then we need to be creative. We have always found it helpful to sit down with our teens, discuss the behavior, brainstorm appropriate consequences and then decide which one to carry out. Adolescents will be less angry when they are a part of the process, so the discipline is more effective.

A third principle of creative discipline is not to make rules you can't enforce. Don't tell a teenager they can't watch TV if they are home alone every afternoon. Don't threaten to take the car away if your teen drives to school and you have no other means of transportation. Rules with inevitable consequences that can be monitored are much more effective.

A little harder, but equally important is a fourth principle: get in touch with your own weaknesses around certain problems before you make unreasonable or illogical rules because of your own unsolved issues in your past. For example, if your father was very demanding, you may be as well with your son or daughter whether you mean to be or not. We all repeat patterns from our past. If a particular issue really seems to get to you, a little soul searching might help uncover the reason why.

A good example of this is the constant disagreements Audrey had at one time with one of our daughters over use of the phone. Her boyfriend was out of state at college and she called him often. Although she paid for the calls with money earned from her part-time job, Audrey continued to hassle her until she realized why. Months earlier her mom, who lived in another state, was widowed. Although Audrey yearned to call her often, she chose not to, to keep the phone bill down. Her mother had since died, and as Audrey watched our daughter choose to spend the money to talk to her boyfriend, she was jealous that she could not re-make the choice to talk more often to her mom. Once she was in touch with this problem, she was able to stop nagging our daughter.

Lastly, creative discipline takes patience and skill. The parent-teen relationship is a complex thing. A third party, like a counselor or church professional, can often see things more clearly. Don't consider it a failure, but an act of love to reach out to someone else, if necessary, to help keep your relationship with your adolescent healthy. The benefits are eternal. The goal of creative discipline is to teach your adolescent self-discipline, but it cannot be accomplished without many mistakes, tears, surprises, and ultimately, joy. In any case, it is well worth the effort.

BALANCE

Balance is another thing our adolescents learn from watching us. Do we balance leisure with work? How do we spend money? In our relationship with them, do we balance criticism and praise? Do we balance time spent to earn them things and our time spent just to be with them? When it comes to our faith, do we spend time at church functions and with our family? Perhaps a good measure for both our parent-teen relationship and our faith life is "the spirit of the law" versus "the letter of the law."

If our teens generally live up to our expectations, can we celebrate that fact as "the spirit of the law" or do we get really upset over one failure and hold tightly to "the letter of the law"? Healthy balance can keep us standing even when the ground gets rather shaky.

TREAT EACH ADOLESCENT AS AN INDIVIDUAL

Each teen has different gifts and a vast array of experiences. It is easy to assume that, having had one teenager, we are equipped for the next, but rules that worked with one seldom work with another. It is tempting to approach a second child with the attitude that we have parenting all figured out, but each child—their friendships, successes and failures, teachers, activities, views of God and their times spent with you—all play a part in making them who they are—totally unique individuals. Wise parents search out these unique gifts and rejoice in the variety. Whether living in an original two parent family, a single parent household, or a blended family, young people will be less likely to compare themselves with others if they know they are appreciated and loved for who they are.

It is uplifting to see God working in each individual life and share what you see with your teenagers. They, too, can see God working, frequently from a different perspective than yours. Sharing those views is real true faith sharing.

ADMIT IT WHEN YOU'RE WRONG

We have often been impressed by the powerful impact it has when a parent says to a teenager, "I'm sorry. I was wrong," or "I didn't understand. Can we try again?" or "I'm sorry I was being crabby. It's not because of you, I'm just worried about something at work." Many breakthroughs in parent-teen relationships have come when mom or dad could admit they were wrong. I find young people very moved by our admission of mistakes and surprisingly understanding. In fact, they respect us more for the times we admit a mistake than for all the times we were right. As a parent of adolescents, it is freeing to not always have to be right. Besides, how can we share our faith life so firmly planted on God's unconditional love and forgiveness if we aren't free enough to say, "I'm sorry"? With teenagers, many fights debate *who* is right. Perhaps more often the issue isn't *who* is right, but *what* is right.

FLEXIBILITY—MODEL GROWTH, NOT RIGIDITY

Every parent of adolescents knows that life, even for one day, is never predictable. The teenage girl who is miserable about a math grade at 2:00 can suddenly be on top of the world at 5:00 when her boyfriend calls. A teenage boy who is excited about receiving his first paycheck from a part-time job at 6:00 can be sullen at 9:00 because his favorite team didn't win the Monday night football game. So, once again, a little flexibility goes a long way. When the 5:00 phone call finally comes for a teenage daughter, you win in lots of ways if you are flexible enough to postpone dinner until 5:30 or eat at 5:00 without demanding her presence. When your son or daughter's coach announces that Parents' Night will be on a night that you were planning to go out, you make your teens feel important if your evening out includes attending Parents' Night.

If you are a very routine person and like to carefully plan the hours of your day, parenting adolescents will be a huge challenge; one of the worst enemies of the parent-teen relationship is rigidity. Parents of teenagers play nurse, tutor, coach, confidant, chauffeur, cook, financier and teacher, and the more easily we can adapt and change hats, the easier life with our adolescents will be. Parents who are "always right" and whose household rules stand inviolate will have more conflicts with their adolescent children than those who are willing to listen to their teenager's views and acknowledge that their view is only one way. Learning to compromise and work out alternatives becomes invaluable while living with teens, especially since our children learn what we model. The fruits of such labor help everyone in the family grow.

PRAISE THE TRUTH; CONDEMN LIES

Adolescents are often convinced that the only way to do what they want without parental opposition is to lie a little bit. It is easier to get permission to go to a party on Friday night if he "forgets" to mention that drinking will be the main activity. If a teen is late for a curfew, she might think it is easier to make up a story than tell the truth, for example, that an argument with a boyfriend led to tears and drawn out conversation with no regard for time. The price of some new name-brand clothing he picked up at the mall will cause less conflict with frugal parents if the price is modified slightly.

If parents want their teenagers to be honest with them, then parents must be truthful with their teens. Young people deplore lies in their relationships with friends, and many adolescent friendships are eliminated over one breach of confidence. As parents, we can capitalize on that and stress how fundamental and basic to our trust is their honesty as well as ours. If we give them our permission (but not our money) to buy expensive clothing, even though we object, they will learn that even though we don't agree with their buying habits, they do not have to lie about it. We can have larger consequences for fabricated stories than for truth, and reassure them that we, too, have had relationship conflicts that leave us unaware of time, and that if they had told the truth about the boyfriend fight, we would have understood and compromised.

We have given our teenagers permission to "check out" a party where drinking was going on with the promise that, if necessary, they would leave and continue the party at our house (amply supplied with pizza and soft drinks), so they wouldn't have to lie about something we knew they would be curious about. Several Saturday nights we have been surprised by a crew of high school students who not only shared our pizza but also their stories of drinking parties. They are often cautious at first and surprised that we know so much about their parties, but eventually they realize that the truth is much more comfortable than lies.

AFFIRMATION

For our young people to be all they can be and build a relationship with God and Church, they must believe in themselves. Adolescents often seem to struggle toward a positive self-image. As one shy, quiet teenager put it, "Gosh, Mrs. Taylor, I have eight bosses a day and all they ever tell me is what I do wrong. I have five different teachers. The English teacher wants my paper typed; the math teacher on loose leaf paper in pencil; the history teacher in a spiral notebook, and they all grade me on how many mistakes I make. Then after school, the coach keeps telling me what I need to do better. At work my boss wants me to work more hours, and when I get home my parents want me to clean my room. Why doesn't anybody tell me what I do right?"

Our young people live in a competitive society and are constantly challenged. Yet the question that really stuck in our minds is, "Why doesn't anybody tell me what I do right?" There is such power to transform through affirmation! Make a point to tell your adolescents what they are doing right and be sure that honest affirmation is a part of every encounter. In our own home, affirmation is much more of a motivator than criticism or directive commands. "I'm so proud of how hard you study," motivates more academic endeavors than, "Have you got your homework done yet?" "Thanks for always being considerate enough to call when you aren't going to make curfew," goes a lot further than, "This is my house and when I say 11:30, I mean 11:30." "You're so good with your little brother. Thanks for playing with him," works better than, "All you think about is yourself. Why don't you play with your little brother once in awhile?" In our family, "I love you" means a lot more than, "Well, we're family, aren't we?" Haven't we all been transformed by kind words or someone who truly believed in us? Haven't we all been inspired and uplifted by a love letter, a special card, or a sincere hug? Affirmation is an often neglected but powerful tool!

CONCLUSION

There are two guiding principles for us as parents. First, we pray a lot. We rely on the Lord. Without abdicating our parental responsibilities, we realize that everything depends on God. Second, we try to realize that there is no single right way to handle any particular situation. We try to remember that each situation and child is unique, so there is no one right way to handle a particular situation. In all things we try to keep Jesus Christ as a our model and to keep our relationship with our teenager as a top priority.

As we conclude our look at parenting skills for faith sharing with adolescents, we need to remember that parenting teenagers is a task that challenges us, exasperates us, makes us proud and gives us innumerable opportunities to love and be loved. How we respond to those opportunities is the key. In an adolescent family, teenagers *and* parents are not always loveable, but people need love the most when it seems they deserve it the least. We can not only survive the adolescent years but also enjoy them if we count on and seek God's grace.

4

SHARING FAITH WITH OLDER ADOLESCENTS

We try to share the Catholic faith with our adolescents one episode at a time, expressing how much it means to us and why, and then gently challenging without making blanket demands. We like to use the word "share" because "sharing" implies a giving—*both* ways. It has been our experience that as we have tried to "pass on" Catholicism to our own adolescents and to the young people we work with, our faith has grown and been re-shaped in many ways as we have talked with teenagers, empathized with their experiences and felt their relationship with the Lord. We have tried to encourage, but not force, our young people to spend time on their faith. We try to encourage a friendship with God and point out that for the two of us that friendship has found many ways to be expressed in the Catholic tradition—especially in the celebration of the Eucharist with our own faith family in our parish.

Marriages that join people of different faiths are increasingly numerous today. While parents may choose to raise their children in the Catholic faith, they should not deprive them of the wonderful opportunity to experience first hand the great worth of other religious traditions. Sharing an appreciation for people of different faiths, ethnic traditions, etc. with young people helps them to grow up more flexible and open to change.

How do parents share the Catholic faith with adolescent children? What are some of the ways we can lead them to believe in the Lord, trust God and ultimately work for the coming of the Kingdom? With two of our four children out of their teens and into their early twenties, we pondered these questions. Since they are all currently quite committed to the Catholic faith, we asked them to tell us how their upbringing had facilitated that. We also asked teens in our parish the same questions. In an attempt to branch out from our own experience, we spent countless hours talking and sharing stories with friends and young people of Hispanic, African-American, Native American, Filipino, Norwegian, Hungarian, Asian and Italian heritage. In our search to discover how Catholicism was transmitted to our friends within their own different ethnic backgrounds, we found more similarities than differences. Based on all of these sources, here are some of the ways to share the Catholic faith with adolescents.

BY EXAMPLE

The first, and perhaps the most difficult and demanding, way to share faith is by example. We can't successfully convince our young people to pray, participate in Eucharist, serve others and be involved in the Church community if we are not setting the example. Adolescents have a keen sense of hypocrisy and "our walk" speaks much louder than "our talk."

Psychologists explain that teenagers are searching for their unique and individual identities. In shopping for one, they will "try on" lots of adult personalities and characteristics. They will view adults and our behavior quite critically. They are unbelievably quick at pointing out the times that "what we do" doesn't live up to "what we say." Sometimes our children's confrontations have led to huge family arguments. Other times, we have been stronger and their observations have been real key moments for modeling what it means to live the Gospel message. Rather than give in to the very human urge to be defensive, we have found it invaluable to accept honest criticism, try to learn from it, grow in positive ways and openly admit that parents are human too.

Another way is to point to grandparents and aunts and uncles as good examples of Christian people. Some of our friends tell of the extensive oral storytelling about family members that present them as models of faith. Saints for them were not just holy people from long ago but beloved people in their own families, real and very human examples to follow.

We have also tried to show lots of concrete ways for our children to live the "spirit of the law" rather than just the "letter of the law." For example, Sunday Mass is a natural issue with young people. In our home, where missing Mass is unacceptable, we have had our share of "discussions" on the topic. We try to instill in our teenagers a sense of gratitude to God and talk often of going to Mass to thank God. There are times, however, when a confrontation over attending Sunday Mass can create more resentment toward Church than that Sunday's attendance is worth. For example, two of our high school daughters were cheerleaders for the second year in a row and were competing intensely for state recognition. All of their after-school extracurricular hours had been devoted to cheerleading; qualifying for state competition was a dream come true. When the final competition was announced and practices were scheduled during the only available gym time, Sunday Mass attendance became a problem. After talking over the situation, we agreed as a family that for this one occasion Sunday Mass could be substituted by a weekday

Mass before school. Our daughters were pleased that we could be so understanding, and through this incident we gave the example of the spirit of weekly liturgy rather than the rigid obligation of Sunday Mass attendance. We also had the opportunity to talk about many things: why we attend Mass every Sunday, an understanding of God and reasons to worship.

IN DAILY ROUTINE AND INTERACTIONS

We are convinced that the style of our daily routine and interactions says (or leaves unsaid) a good deal about our faith. Just watching and living our daily routine teaches our young people our values. They learn how we use time, how we eat, how we manage or mismanage money, how we handle or avoid conflict and many other things. Most of these things speak to them about our faith life. They learn how we pray, how we are involved or uninvolved in church, how we think about and relate to God. This style of living communicates that faith is not saved for Sundays; it permeates everyday life.

Mealtime prayer can say a lot about how we pray. For years our family said the traditional, "Bless us, O Lord, and these Thy gifts" before dinner. By the time our children reached adolescence, though, this prayer was extremely routine and often quite meaningless. The words were often mumbled as the food was passed, leading us to reconsider how we prayed at dinner. We tried lots of different things to revitalize that short prayer time: we took turns leading the prayer by bringing a favorite poem or prayer to share; sharing and reading aloud our favorite Scripture passage; and reading from a booklet from our local Christian bookstore. All of these were minimally successful, but not what we really wanted. It wasn't until we tried a more routine and simple prayer that it began to feel more like a sincere effort to be in touch with God.

We decided to begin our dinner time with shared and personal intentions voiced aloud so we could all remember one another's intentions when we were apart. This mealtime prayer seemed to catch on well. We didn't have to remember any written material, it was routine enough to become a habit, and it gave us lots of material for further conversation as we asked one another questions about the people and situations that made up the content of our prayer. We have shared intentions at dinner time long enough that extended family members, co-workers and even visiting boyfriends feel comfortable with it now. On special days like birthdays or holidays we still add, "Bless us, O Lord..." The messages we sent to our adolescents as we worked to re-vitalize our routine prayer were important: that (1) we value praying together each day, even if only for a few moments; (2) when prayer is only mumbled words, rather than a sincere effort to be in contact with the Lord, it needs to be re-worked; (3) praying for the intentions of others and in community is important ("When two or three are gathered in my name..."); and (4) prayer should come from the heart and be a real conversation with the Lord.

The ethnic heritage and traditions that are part of our family life also provide opportunities for celebrating God's continuing presence to us. Ethnic holidays and holy days, celebrated as a family or with the larger community, provide discovery of God's love for us not just through words, but also through food and dress, songs and games. Getting in touch with the traditions that are part of our personal ethnic background helps us experience, as a family, how God's love has been shared with the family members who came before us. Sharing in the ethnic customs and traditions of people of other races and nationalities helps us expand our understanding of God—and grow in appreciation of others.

A lot of other routine things speak of our faith. Our language often indicates our respect or lack of respect for the Lord. What we react to—and don't react to—both send strong messages to our teenagers. Our comments as we read the daily newspaper and watch TV tell our young people a lot about what we value. Certain newspaper articles and love scenes and acts of violence on TV have led to lengthy discussions in our home because we have found these daily occurrences are natural moments to insert powerful value statements.

Our daily interactions with one another also tell our young people how we really practice our faith. Is there kindness, courtesy and respect in our conversations and interactions with each other? Are we truly forgiving when the need arises or are we unable to let go of past hurts? Either way we are imprinting messages about reconciliation in the "memory banks" of our young people's minds. As we interact with our adolescents, are there lots of invitations and loving challenges or only "mandatory" obligations? In these ways and myriads of others, our daily routines and interactions with our teenagers have much to do with transmitting and sharing our faith.

TALKING ABOUT VALUES

Every time our adolescents ask us, "Why?" we have an opportunity to share the values of our faith. In the many discussions that follow that often-asked question, there can be times of real value clarification and faith sharing. For instance, when one of our daughters asked us, "Why should I declare my waitress tips on my income tax? No one else does," we had a meaningful discussion about honesty versus cheating. "Why do we save so much money for college and drive such beat up cars?" started a dialogue about the value of education and the over-rated status symbol of a new sports car. And, "Why do we have to go to Grandma's? It's so boring" opened a conversation about the value of family as a community of which you'll always be a part. When teens ask, "Why can't we stay overnight in a hotel suite after the post-prom picnic? It's a whole bunch of couples, not just us two," you can use the occasion to talk about relationships and sexuality as a God-given gift with responsibilities attached. And so on.

In addition to all of the daily opportunities we have, Christmas is an especially powerful time of the year to contrast the values of the Gospel and the values of a materialistic society. Some of our more lengthy and emotional family discussions have centered around the expectations of Christmas and holiday spending, and two family habits have emerged from them. The first is that each time you receive a new piece of clothing, you can hang it in your closet only after you have removed another to share with others who have less. I realized this had become a family habit when Christmas time as well as each birthday celebration found us automatically giving clothes to our friend who was working in a mission for the poor. The second habit is that rather than buying an expensive gift for someone we care about, we use our own creative talents to make something as an expression of love. Our house is now full of homemade posters and collages, hand-painted picture frames, stationary decorated with calligraphy, special poems, hand-painted sweatshirts and a cherished collection of handwritten "love letters." One of our daughters even bought us a new telephone-address book and lovingly copied over all the names and numbers from our old torn book. What a gift of time! And what a message that Christmas wasn't meant to be a time of spending, but a time of loving!

Special events and milestones in our life as a family, like anniversaries and graduations, family moves and job changes, also provide a time to talk about family values and how we try to live them out. Similar special moments are a natural part of some ethnic traditions, for example, the *quince años* or fifteenth birthday celebration shared by families of Mexican descent or the celebration of *Kwanzaa* shared by families of African American heritage. Each of these celebrations provides an opportunity for families to share their hopes, values and beliefs with one another.

In all of our discussions about values we have tried to encourage our children to ask themselves two questions when making a choice or decision: (1) Will this be a life-giving decision for all involved or will it drain life from those it affects? (2) Is this a choice or a decision for people or for things? How will my choices and actions affect the people around me? Am I just accumulating more things? Dialogues such as these with our adolescents have been a key way for us to share the values of our faith.

CRISES DISCUSSED
IN THE LIGHT OF FAITH

Faith is shared more intentionally in our home whenever we are faced with a crisis. Adolescents seem more tuned into our actions and our thoughts when we must deal with problems. They watch and question, trying to understand and to learn coping skills all at the same time. It's a key time to display the strength that our faith gives us and also use the experience as a time for special learning.

When an extended family member was suffering through a painful divorce, our adolescents were very much aware and often asked questions about the Church's teachings on marriage and divorce. When a high schooler in our neighborhood became pregnant, it opened many discussions about her fate, abortion and the sacredness of our sexuality. When one of our daughters broke up with a boyfriend, our teens were much more attuned to conversations about faithfulness and learning from loss. When our oldest daughter was married, there were lots of dinner time discussions about what qualities she chose in picking her husband. There were also discussions about virginity and how hard it was to wait for marriage and even about the special strength we get from the sacrament of Matrimony.

When my brother died of a sudden heart attack at age 39, the night before Thanksgiving, we prayed and talked for days about being thankful for the gift of life, however short. We talked about death and eternal life, about what living is meant to be, and about our Catholic faith and the comfort it afforded us as we mourned his loss. My brother was a sculptor and an outdoorsman, and the last statue he made was of a giant eagle with wings extended. At his funeral, the eagle was carried out behind his casket as the choir sang, "I will raise you up on eagle's wings." What a powerful image and a powerful time for sharing our faith! Crises are important times for faith sharing.

CONTACTS WITH OTHER FAITH-FILLED ADULTS

Often in families with adolescents, parents are the adults least able to convey a desired message to teenage sons or daughters. Your choice of pasta for dinner may be quickly rejected in favor of frozen pizza until an admired athletic coach suggests pasta for "carbohydrate loading" before a big game. Parents' ideas are presumed wrong until proven otherwise by a trusted friend or a boyfriend's mother. Being their parent makes you, in the eyes of your adolescent, one of the last people from whom ever to seek advice. With those strikes against us it's no wonder contacts with other faith-filled adults are important in our teenager's development.

For that reason, among others, having good friends within our Church community has many benefits. Our church involvement also makes it possible for us to meet people of other cultures and traditions. The church is large enough to include many different traditions and approaches to worship. Meeting others who share our faith, but express it in different ways, enriches us all. Our teenagers are exposed in our home and through parish programs to adults who have similar Christian values. Sunday liturgies and other special times at church are more than just times to fill the pew for an hour out of obligation, but times to see friends and feel a real sense of belonging that is so important to teenagers. Our adolescents are always willing to attend liturgy on Thanksgiving morning, for instance, because as one of my high schoolers put it, "It's the best Mass of the whole year 'cause everyone who goes really wants to. And we see so many people we know." Typically at the end of that Mass we spend a half hour afterward greeting friends and catching up with their college-age children who are home for the holiday. For an adolescent with an enormous need for belonging, this time of true friendship associated with church is a real plus.

Because of the emotional complexity of the parent-teen relationship, other faith-filled adults can often better challenge our teenagers and are often a source of comfort and advice when we cannot be. Since young people are searching for and struggling to find their own identity, they often "try on" the personalities of those around them. Why not give them a variety of adult Catholic Christians to consider in their "shopping"?

EXPERIENCE IN PEACE AND JUSTICE ACTIVITIES

Another avenue for sharing faith is involvement in peace and justice activities such as soup kitchens, caring for the elderly, etc. Our young people are not moved by pious words about social responsibility but by looking into the eyes of another human being and seeing the pain they have endured. Our children have established a real concern for the poor and oppressed not from our conversations or sermons but from actual experiences.

As teenagers they went with us to a widow's home for a Saturday "cleaning bee." They mowed the lawn for an elderly widower in our neighborhood and were moved by his tearful gratitude. They have volunteered in soup kitchens and shelters for the homeless through school and youth group activities. They have visited local nursing homes and monopolized our dinner conversations with their stories of the elderly there. As some have graduated from high school we have seen these experiences broaden. Our daughter joined the Jesuit Volunteer Corps and worked for a year in a shelter for battered women. Another, who loves children, has worked summers in an Appalachian children's camp. A third daughter left her graduation ceremony and stayed up late to pack for a trip to Guatemala to work with the poor there. What a change from her junior high years when new possessions and name-brand clothes were so important to her! We knew her outlook had changed radically when we asked for suggestions for a graduation gift and she answered, "I have more than I need. How about helping me pay for a plane ticket to Central America so I can go serve there?" Her earlier exposure to the faces of the poor had reaped a special harvest.

As our young people today search for their place in the world and experiment with different ways to live and relate to others, peace and justice experiences can change their views and behaviors in powerful ways. It can also change their faith life from an intellectual "believing" to an actual "trusting" in the Lord's guidance and a very real "doing". It is then that the words of the Gospel become the foundation for actions that build the Kingdom. "Whatsoever you do to the least of my brethren, that you do unto me..."

PRAYER

In our attempts to share faith with our adolescents there is a feeling that after we have done our best, it is somehow out of our hands. Our teenagers will be exposed to lots of experiences and people beyond our horizons. They will make their own choices and decisions; some we will be happy about, some will be a disappointment. To help us accept this, we go to the Lord and pray for his help. Like most parents we pray not only for the physical and emotional well-being of our children, but also for their faith life. We pray daily that our children will grow up close to the Lord. We dig down into our own faith to pull up our belief in the power of prayer: "Ask and you shall receive..."

A key to sharing faith with our children is not only praying for them but teaching them the power and skills of prayer. When they were little we gathered each night in our youngest child's bedroom for prayers. As the years passed and bedtimes varied, we tried many other ways to give witness to the importance of prayer. We shared special prayer times during Advent around our Advent wreath; we read children's bible stories in the evening; we read and discussed Scripture passages.

As our home filled with teenagers involved in school athletics, part-time jobs and endless phone conversations, our organized prayer times became fewer and fewer, and we found ourselves searching for a new way to pray together as a family. After reviewing the family calendar, we discovered that Monday nights were fairly empty of outside activities, so we posted an invitation on the refrigerator—"All Are Invited to Family Prayer Time; Monday Night in the Family Room at approximately 9:30 PM." (After Monday night football, of course.) It truly was an invitation; no one was forced to be there. Our goal was to make it special enough that siblings would convince each other to come. Sometimes we sang while our daughter played the guitar; sometimes we shared a Scripture story and our thoughts about it; sometimes we recited a rosary. Each time we ended with shared intentions as each family member held a candle, voiced their prayer aloud and then passed the candle on to the next person. We did not always have everyone present, but we did have some special and uplifting prayer times together. I trust that our struggle for regular prayer time will be unending, but I also trust that our young people have taken some powerful messages about our prayer times for and with them. "When two or three are gathered in my name, I am there...."

INTEREST AND INVOLVEMENT IN PARISH

Sharing faith with adolescents means sharing in their faith experiences: their sacramental preparation, their retreat times, their religion classes. If your child is being confirmed in high school, you can use this opportunity to help him or her prepare for the sacrament. For example, most Confirmation programs have a service requirement. This can be an opportunity to talk with your adolescent about the difference between completing one service project and living a life of service. Choosing sponsors and a saint's name can be a mere formality or an enriching time to share stories of the saints and those who have influenced our lives and our faith.

Teens in a Catholic school or parish program usually have the opportunity to make a retreat, and being involved and interested in this can be very rewarding. In a world full of TVs, tape decks, telephones and hundreds of other distractions from God's messages, a retreat can be a very special time for an adolescent. Many retreat programs involve the parents by writing letters, by attending liturgy or by chaperoning. Retreats are popular with young people and truly become a time they "re-treat" themselves to a friendship with the Lord.

Your teens may also attend organized religious discussions and classes. The subject matter of those classes can add much to your discussions of faith at home and enrich your own faith as well. One of our favorite religious education lessons is a session in which Jesus Christ is put on trial. Each student takes a role: judge, prosecuting attorney, defense lawyer, Mary, Peter, a Pharisee, Mary Magdalene, etc. The proceedings at this "trial" filled many of our discussions at home with religious eduction material and opened our eyes to new ways of looking at a familiar story.

Since peers have a major influence on the decisions of adolescents, it pays to have your teenagers involved with other young people who are part of a parish youth ministry or a Catholic high school campus ministry. Research has shown that young people who are involved with their parish are much more likely to continue some involvement after they leave home. If your parish has an active youth ministry, you can encourage your teenagers to take part in their activities. If not, you can help form one. Most parish youth ministries are created and maintained by interested parishioners.

PARENT EDUCATION

Our young people cannot commit their lives to something they do not know, so an education in our faith becomes important for our children as well as for us. As parents we can't expect our adolescents to learn about the faith if we are still walking around with an outdated view of Catholicism. Just as our household appliances are regularly updated when they no longer serve us, so should we update our faith. Adult education programs, religious seminars, parish missions, Lenten lectures and an abundance of Catholic reading material are only a few of the ways we can update our faith knowledge. Whether it's courses, movies or magazines, the important thing is our constant willingness to re-think, re-learn and re-commit our lives to our faith. As our children witness our learning, they will more easily accept their own religious education.

CONCLUSION

How do we share faith with adolescents? Are there "secrets" to sharing our Catholic faith? As young children, our offspring took part in our faith activities without question. As they have become adolescents, and we have met resistance, we have tried to gradually lessen our demands and increase our invitations. Sometimes it feels extremely risky to leave adolescents a choice (about anything!), and sometimes it is painful to watch them put God and their spiritual life at the bottom of their list of priorities. Sometimes it's a source of conflict, but equally often it's uplifting to see the fantastic choices they can make to live their faith in Jesus Christ. Sometimes it's humbling to share their prayers and experience their relationship with the Lord. When all of these beautiful ideals seem impossible and the "nitty gritty" negatives seem overwhelming, we try to remind ourselves of the good things God has accomplished through our parenting, beginning with the creation of a new life. Even though we have often not been as good parents as we hoped to be and succumbed to very human (and very loud) "family feuds," we are family. We've often relayed to our adolescents the words of the song—"All I ask of you is forever to remember me as loving you." In the discouraging moments, we try to remind ourselves that Jesus always invited, never demanded. In the wonderful moments we celebrate God's grace and remind ourselves that with the faith we share and the relationships we build, God will guide us into the future.

5

STRATEGIES AND ACTIVITIES

SHARING THE CATHOLIC FAITH STORY

Families play a key role in sharing the values and beliefs of the Catholic community. This is done when:

- all family members, especially adults, continue to grow in their own faith through reading, informal discussion or participation in parish or community educational programs and share their learnings with one another;

■ families participate in intergenerational catechetical experiences, gathering with other families to learn, grow and live the Catholic faith;

■ families make the connection between their life experiences and faith values, drawing on the rich resources of Scripture, Catholic Tradition and the faith traditions found in their ethnic heritage;

■ families participate together in the sacramental preparation of individual family members;

■ families recognize the impact of media and learn to evaluate media critically in light of the life-giving values of the Catholic Christian faith.

The following activities provide examples of how the Catholic faith story can be shared meaningfully by families during the adolescent years.

ACTIVITY 1. SHARING STORIES OF FAITH

As important as faith may be, it isn't a normal topic of dinner conversation in most families with adolescents. Most often young people (and their parents) need a bit of assistance and structure in order to move faith to the forefront in family discussions. This activity takes a story sharing approach to discussing faith. It helps young people and their parents articulate why faith is important to them and how they find it in the ordinary experiences of their life. The process is a simple one that lends itself to use throughout the year:

Reflect: Use any or all of the following open-ended sentences as a starting point for a family discussion on faith. Choose the questions together. Give people some quiet time to reflect on or write out their responses before moving to discussion.

Something that is really different about Catholicism today, compared to 20 or 30 years ago is....

In my experience as a teenager, attending Mass on Sunday.....

A person who has really influenced my faith life.....
   She/He influenced me by.....
As a child, I was taught to pray.....
   Now I pray.....
Something I love about being part of the Church.....
A difficulty I have with the Church.....
A time in my life when I really needed God was.....
When I think about Jesus.....
I believe faith is important because.....

Share: Invite family members to share their reflections with one another. Some may find it difficult to share aloud the first time or two, so patience is essential. Just talking about faith together reflects its importance in your life and offers family members a chance to rethink how they see or experience faith.

A few hints on dialoguing about faith with adolescents:

- Allow and encourage young people to be honest with themselves and with you about where they are at in their faith journey. For some young people faith is a certainty. For others it is a real struggle. Both faith stances can be very real. Both need to be respected.

- For many young people faith is most tangible when seen through the perspective of personal relationships and/or values. Raising the issue of who and what they believe in, and why, can be a fruitful starting point for discussions of faith.

- Be flexible in your conversations about faith. Discussing issues and questions of immediate concern to young people, even when the issues do not appear to be explicitly religious, can be a prelude to an encounter with the deeper questions of personal faith.

Pray: Close your sharing of faith stories with a simple, spontaneous prayer, or ask a family member in advance to come prepared with a brief closing prayer.

Learn More About It:

Flynn, Eileen and Gloria Thomas. *Living Faith: An Introduction to Theology.* Kansas City, MO: Sheed & Ward, 1989.

Rohr, Richard and Joseph Martos. *Why Be Catholic? Understanding Our Experience and Tradition.* Cincinnati: St. Anthony Messenger Press, 1989.

ACTIVITY 2. CONVERSATIONS ABOUT CAREER CHOICES

In *A Century of Catholic Social Teaching: A Common Heritage, A Continuing Challenge,* the U.S. bishops remind us that "work is more than a way to make a living; it is an expression of our dignity and a form of continuing participation in God's creation." Young people give a lot of time to considerations of job and career and the schooling needed to get there. They explore their talents and skills, survey the personnel needs of business and industry locally and nationally, check out school and training options, weigh potential job demands against salary and benefits and try to come up with a mix of ingredients that will help them meet the criteria they've established for personal and professional success. Too often this process takes place without conscious consideration of the values questions involved in career decisions.

As older adolescents wrestle with the questions of career direction, sharing some key questions with them can challenge them to reflect on the call to live out faith in our daily life commitments. These questions could be asked by a parent, a relative, a trusted adult friend or a parish youth minister. If, for example, a young person has decided on a career in health care, the following questions might be asked:

- Why health care? What will it do for you, and what will it enable you to do for others?

- What aspect of health care are you looking into and why?

- Who is most in need of health care today in our country or world? How will your training help you respond to their needs?

- What schools are you exploring? What kind of on-the-job training do they provide? With what kind of clientele would you be working?

- What languages might you need to be able to do health care well in the cities, suburbs and rural regions of our country? Is there space in your course work for a language course or two?

- What are health care salaries and benefits like? What kind of lifestyle do you expect to live? How much do you expect to be able to share with others?

- How could your job skills be used in a volunteer capacity? Do you see volunteering in your future? How can you start preparing now to be a more competent volunteer in the future?

- What can we learn from the life of Jesus about the Christian call to healing?

Regardless of the job or profession, similar questions should fit. Helping young people work through the answers can be a great service to them and to the world.

ACTIVITY 3. D.E.C.I.D.E.—A PROCESS FOR MORAL DECISION MAKING

Adolescents face many pressured, moral choices. At times the moral choices they make bring them into conflict with their parents. This activity provides a framework in which adolescents and their parents can discuss the elements that go into making sound moral choices.

D—Determine all the influences on your moral decision.

Describe and list all the things that are part of the dilemma or problem at hand or that will influence your choices: reason or intellect, family, feelings, freedom, friends, media, beliefs and values, authority figures, society, cultural heritage, past experiences, Catholic faith, relationship with Jesus Christ.

E—Educate yourself further on the problem or question.

List all the ways possible to become better informed about the problem or question at stake. Select the ways that seem like they will offer you the most knowledge and help. Call to mind Jesus' law of love and the moral laws and norms the Church teaches. Spend time thinking and reasoning about options rather than simply acting on impulse and feelings.

C—Consult reliable authorities.

Talk with those persons who will provide sound advice, new insights, opinions that might not perfectly fit with your own, or the kind of care and support you will need. Pay particular attention to what you can learn from Jesus, the Bible, the Church and those life-giving people on whom you rely, like your family. Make good use of the insight or wisdom of others and your own personal reason to decide what is right, what is wrong and what would be the most appropriate action. There are certain core Catholic values which should play a part each time we use the process.

I—In prayer, ask for God's help.

Pray for guidance. Spend time in prayer, alone or with others like your family, before your choice is made. Be open to the Spirit of Jesus and how it will lead you and support you as you decide. What would Jesus do in this situation? Ask Jesus to help you be faithful to his Law of Love. Seek the Lord's guidance in Scripture. Ask the Holy Spirit to make you a loving person—helping you to do what is right and reject what is wrong. Listen to what your conscience is saying about the situation. Ask God to be with you in your decision and after it has taken place.

D—Decide; make your moral choice and act on it.
List all the pros and cons in the situation. Look at each reason and decide how important it is. Be sure to reflect on what values are at stake in your pros and cons. How will it influence your life and future, your relationships with other people, and your relationship with Jesus? Using your assessment of the pros and cons go ahead and make a decision. List the ways you will carry out your decision. Identify who you will inform about your decision. Now you are ready to act on your moral choice. Act with the knowledge and faith that you have worked hard to inform your conscience and make the best choice you can.

E—Evaluate your decision.
We evaluate decisions by taking time to think over some important questions, such as: Did anyone get hurt as a result of my choice? Which relationships did it help or did it damage? What basic values were at stake in my decision? How did I act on the core Catholic norms and laws? What have been the chief consequences for myself, my future, others? Am I proud of my choice? Did I do the right thing? Did I really follow my informed Christian conscience?

[Excerpted from *Moral Decision-Making* by Audrey Taylor (New York: Sadlier, 1988).]

Learn More About It:

Marinelli, Anthony. *Conscience and Catholic Faith*. Mahwah, NJ: Paulist Press, 1991.
I Can't Decide! What Should I Do? Boys Town Video for Parents. A 15-minute video available from Don Bosco Multimedia.

CELEBRATING RITUALS AND PRAYING TOGETHER

Families provide a sense of rhythm and celebration to their faith life by celebrating unique family rituals and participating in the ritual life of the parish community. This is done when:

- families celebrate the many ways that the sacred is revealed in their shared life through home rituals focused on ordinary family events, important milestones in family life, liturgical seasons and appropriate civic holidays;

- families regularly participate in the Sunday Eucharistic assembly;

- families actively participate in parish rituals that support and complement their home rituals and celebrations;

- all family members actively participate in the preparation and celebration of the sacramental rites of passage of family members through in-home activities and participation in parish programs;

- families reclaim, affirm and celebrate their own ethnic rituals and traditions and participate in cultural and ethnic celebrations offered by the parish community and the wider Church and civic community.

Families encourage the development of a family prayer life and involve family members in the prayer life of the parish community. This is done when:

- parents and adult family members continue to grow by devoting time and care to their relationship with God through spiritual development programs and resources;

- families develop a pattern of family prayer which nurtures faith and sustains the family during times of change or crisis;

- parents help their children to pray in age-appropriate ways;

- families join with others in the parish community for prayer and support;

- families draw upon their ethnic prayer traditions in creating their family prayer pattern and draw on the cultural and ethnic prayer traditions of the extended family, parish and wider church community;

- parents encourage participation of family members in age-specific spiritual development programs and prayer experiences/services and connect an individual's experience in these programs to the family's prayer life.

The following activities provide practical examples of how families can share together in ritual and prayer during the adolescent years.

ACTIVITY 1. A RITUAL OF FAMILY COMMITMENT

Sometimes, in the rush of different schedules and activities family members can forget the special gift they are to one another as family. This simple ritual provides an example of how families can recall the specialness of their relationship and recommit themselves to growing together as family. The ritual can be used during a holiday season when family members are spending quality time together, in conjunction with a church feast, e.g., the Feast of the Holy Family, or at any time during the year when a reminder of the importance of family seems appropriate. Use the prayer service as outlined below or adapt it together to fit the specific needs and interests of your family.

Leader: Father, we gather today as members of a family with a past history and a future hope. We celebrate and proclaim the sacredness of our family, even in its imperfections and brokenness. We recommit ourselves to be a family which is willing to pray, love, forgive, and to share with one another and with all your people.

Each one of us can make a difference in our family this year, by undertaking the following promises. Please repeat each promise after me. (OR—*Statements may be phrased as questions, with family members responding "I do."*)

I promise to help my family become a loving community for each member and for the world in which we live. *(Repeat)*

I promise to do my best:

    . . . to pray with and for my family. *(Repeat)*

    . . . to share with my family through word and example.

    . . . to celebrate and preserve the rituals and traditions of my family.

    . . . to show love and affection through word and touch.

    . . . to forgive and to reconcile.

    . . . to communicate honestly and openly.

    . . . to freely share my time and treasures.

    . . . to do my share of the work.

    . . . to be hospitable to all who enter into our home.

    . . . and to always show respect for each family member.

Leader: Let us bow our heads and pray for our family. May God strengthen our resolve to enrich the life of our family. May God reconcile any hurts or broken relationships in our family. May God give us the courage to help our family grow as a community of life and love. May the peace of the Lord be with us always.

All: Amen.

Leader: Let us now offer one another a sign of peace to symbolize the commitments we have made to being life-giving members of this family.

As a sign of commitment to one another, family members may share a festive meal, with each family member contributing something to the meal (food, decoration, music, etc.).

Learn More About It:

Roberto, John, ed. *Family Rituals and Celebrations.* New Rochelle, NY: Don Bosco Multimedia, 1992. (This volume is a collection of rituals and celebrations that you can use or adapt.)

ACTIVITY 2. A FAMILY GRADUATION CELEBRATION

Because graduation is the culmination of so much that is intensely personal, one family invented a tradition that has become significant for them, the personal diploma.

The personal diploma began as something to complement the institutional diploma received by their graduating son. In contrast to the somber black lettering on white parchment, their family diploma was elaborately decorated with a colorful and intricate border interspersed with symbols of their son's involvement in family, school and community activities. Family members wrote the diploma text themselves and found a local artist to design their diploma.

The diploma was "conferred" in a special family celebration that incorporated Scripture, prayer and story telling.

The Scripture passage chosen was Ecclesiastes 3:1-8, a reading that reminds us there is a time for everything—and that God is with us in all seasons, including times of family change.

The prayers used during the service expressed the family's thanks and hopes for the graduate. Use the following prayer or create one of your own:

Parent/Leader:
>   (Name) you are a unique creation,
>   a person blessed by God with life,
>   a person called, in love, to grow

and to share your gifts with others.

We come together today to celebrate your accomplishments,
to reflect on who you are for us
and to share our dreams for your future.

May your graduation day be filled with happiness and joy.

We rejoice in who you are for us as a family, calling to mind especially your gifts of _____ and
_____.

(Family members can be invited to share comments and stories here that speak of the uniqueness and giftedness of the graduate)

May God continue to bless you and challenge you.
May you always be surrounded by people who support and love you.
May you grow more fully into the man/woman that God wants you to be, and that the world so desperately needs.

We ask this today, in hope and expectation that God will continue the great things already begun in you. Amen.

The family graduation ceremony closed with shared hugs and a special meal.

ACTIVITY 3. STEPFAMILIES: STRENGTHENING TIES THROUGH PRAYER AND RITUAL

By establishing their own traditions and rituals, stepfamilies build family bonds and create a family identity of their own. Family traditions shared year after year build a sense of permanence and continuity for family members. They provide shared memories of enjoyable times, spent together, that can sustain family members through the periods of change and conflict that are part of life in all families.

If children divide their holiday time between two different homes, or enter a blended family with established holiday traditions and rituals, it may be difficult to negotiate new and meaningful ways of celebrating the major holidays and holy days of the year. But that doesn't stop families from creating alternative celebrations or expanding their repertoire of family rituals.

Christmas spent with one parent (or set of parents) can be supplemented with a special "Little Christmas" celebration on the feast of the Epiphany, January 6—the twelfth day of Christmas celebrated with much fanfare and joy in the countries of Latin America. Or stepfamilies can celebrate the first snowfall (or first flower of spring) in a unique, family way.

Special dates in the life of the stepfamily can also be celebrated in prayer and ritual. Consider, for example, a family celebration of the wedding anniversary or an annual remembrance of the first night the stepfamily came together in a home of their own.

Consciously choosing dates and events to celebrate that are different from those already celebrated by individual family members can help build new relationships (without denying the old) and build a pool of shared experiences and fun times to help families move forward into the future.

ENRICHING FAMILY RELATIONSHIPS

Families encourage the individual growth of family members and the development of meaningful relationships within and beyond the family. This is done when:

- parents grow in their understanding of the parenting skills needed at each stage of the family life cycle;

- families work to improve their communications, decision-making and problem-solving skills;

- families work at and enjoy spending quality time together;

■ families participate in intergenerational, family activities which build community among family members and between families in the parish community;

■ married couples consciously work at enriching their marriage relationship;

■ single, divorced, separated or widowed adults work at enriching their lives and relationships through programs, support groups, and resources that address their specific needs;

■ families seek support and counseling during times of loss, sudden change, unexpected crises, problems and family or personal transitions.

The following activities provide practical examples of how family relationships can be nurtured and enriched during the adolescent years.

ACTIVITY 1. PARENTING AND ENCOURAGEMENT

One of the key roles of parents is to encourage and enable the growth of their children. Parenting by encouraging builds self-esteem through focusing attention on young people's resources. Encouraging parents look for the positive sides to their children's traits. They support their children efforts to pursue their own goals, provided, of course, that the goals are reasonable and socially acceptable. Unlike praise, which rewards achievement and can foster competition or fear of failure, encouragement rewards effort and improvement, fostering cooperation and confidence. Consider the following strategies for encouraging the growth of adolescents in your family:

■ have positive expectations about what they can do and be;

■ emphasize the process (of living and learning), not just the product;

- give them responsibility;

- show appreciation for their contributions at home;

- ask for their opinions and suggestions;

- encourage their participation in decision making;

- show confidence in their judgement;

- respect their attempts;

- accept their mistakes;

- develop alternative ways of viewing situations.

Learn More About It:

Dinkmeyer, Don and Gary D. McKay. *The Parent's Guide: Systematic Training for Effective Parenting of Teens.* Circle Pines, MN: American Guidance Service, 1983

ACTIVITY 2. STRENGTHENING THE RELATIONSHIP BETWEEN PARENT AND TEEN

During adolescence the parenting role begins to shift in major ways. As young people begin to take more personal responsibility for their own lives and grow increasingly independent, parents are faced with the task of restructuring their relationships with teens. Part of that restructuring involves laying the foundation for a new adult-to-adult relationship with teens that will endure into the future. Working to build a new, adult relationship with your teen does not mean you have to set aside your parenting responsibilities, but it can help you look on those responsibilities in a new way. As the new relationship grows, your influence also grows, based not on control but on mutual respect. The following simple approaches are offered as steps to shifting and strengthening a new relationship between parent and teen:

- Make time to talk with and listen to each other.

- Do things together that feel good and allow the time needed to build a new relationship.
- Pay attention to how well the two of you are getting along, ironing out problems together as they arise.
- Make sure you are both getting your needs met, while remaining sensitive to your teen's needs.

The process is simple enough. Relate to your teen as you would relate to any good friend. Stay with the relationship and watch it grow.

Learn More About It:

Kirshenbaum, Mira and Charles Foster. *Parent/Teen Breakthrough: The Relationship.* New York: A Plume Book, 1991.

ACTIVITY 3. ENRICHING RELATIONSHIPS IN BLENDED FAMILIES

Families today come in different sizes, shapes and configurations. Many young people live at least a portion of their lives in blended families, sharing their home with one biological parent, a step parent and a mixture of biological and step siblings. Blended families are a special and different kind of family. While parents and teens in blended families are similar in some ways to parents and teens in other kinds of families, their journey can also be quite different. Adults who carry the dual role of biological and stepparent can feel like jugglers—attempting to develop new relationships with stepchildren while nurturing established relationships with their biological offspring. Young people in blended families can feel alone, or conversely, overwhelmed by their struggle to maintain relationships with two, three or four different parents. In *Strengthening Your Stepfamily*, Elizabeth Einstein and Linda Albert suggest the following guidelines for easing the adjustment of parents into stepfamily life:

For stepparents:

■ Seek support—from your spouse, friends, minister or rabbi, other stepparents.

■ Be there for your stepchildren, but allow them time to learn to trust and respect you.

■ Respect the strong bond that exists between your spouse and children. Allow them plenty of time together and avoid interfering where issues are not your concern.

For biological parents:

■ Include your new spouse in your existing family unit, but let relationships develop at their own pace.

■ Be supportive, ready to listen and discuss difficulties.

■ Encourage a cooperative spirit between your spouse and the children's other biological parent.

For both of you:

■ Explore your parenting styles and take classes together to develop problem-solving and discipline skills.

■ Work out ways for your stepfamily to communicate: family meetings, bulletin boards, complaint and compliment pots, regular planned activities.

■ Talk about feelings. Airing them aloud diminishes their power.

■ Be patient, allowing plenty of time for family members to work through their many differences.

■ Make your couple relationship a priority. Remember, when parents are happy, children feel more secure.

Learn More About It:

Bonkowski Ph.D., Sara. *Teens Are NON Divorceable*. Chicago: ACTA Publications, 1990.

Clubb, Angela Neumann. *Love in the Blended Family*. Deerfield Beach FL: Health Communications, Inc., 1991.

Einstein, Elizabeth and Linda Albert. *Strengthening Your Stepfamily*. Circle Pines, MN: American Guidance Service, 1986.

Getzoff, Ann and Carolyn McClenahan. *Step Kids: A Survival Guide for Teenagers in Step Families*. New York: Walker and Company, 1984.

RESPONDING TO THOSE IN NEED AND RELATING TO THE WIDER COMMUNITY

Families respond to the gospel call to service by reaching out in compassion to those in need. This is done when:

- family members model the gospel values of respect for human dignity, compassion, justice and service to others in their relationships with each other and with others in the community;

- families learn about justice issues and the needs of others;

- family members participate together in parish and community service programs geared to their interests and abilities;

- families discuss how the needs of others, locally and globally, affect their life as a family;

- families joins with others in society to alleviate the suffering of those in need and change the structures that allow injustice and inequality to continue.

Families work to better understand the world they live in and make it a better place for all people. This is done when:

- families model hospitality, opening their home to others, showing how God's love is communicated through family life;

- families grow in appreciation of their own ethnic or cultural heritage;
- families takes part in parish and community events that help them understand the life and history of people of different cultures and nations, and value cultural diversity as a special gift from God;
- families recognize their connectedness with and reliance upon others at all levels of life and grow in their appreciation for interdependence;
- families learn about and join in actions with others who share a common vision and approach for improving life in the community .

The following activities provide examples of how the families with adolescents can reach out together in response to the needs of the local and wider community.

ACTIVITY 1. A WORD OF FAMILY CONCERN

Write a joint letter to your state or congressional legislators about an issue of concern to your family. If the letter is about an issue currently on the agenda for legislative consideration, it will carry additional weight. By following the bill's progress through the legal process, the entire family will get a better idea of how a bill becomes law and how people can let their voices be heard around on of equality and justice.

Learn More About It:

Lewis, Barbara A. *The Kid's Guide to Social Action*. Minneapolis: Free Spirit Publishing Inc., 1991.
McGinnis, Kathleen and James. *Parenting for Peace and Justice*. Maryknoll, NY: Orbis Books, 1981.
Salzman, Marian and Teresa Reisgies. *150 Ways Teen Can Make a Difference*. Princeton, NJ: Peterson's Guides, Inc., 1991.

ACTIVITY 2. FAMILY FINANCES

Talk through finances regularly so that all family members have a better idea about what is involved in budgeting and how much things really cost. Decide how and when major purchases will be made. Discuss together how the family shares its resources with others, how much of the family income goes to church, charitable and social change groups, and how the money is divided.

ACTIVITY 3. JUSTICE ISSUES
AS PLAYED OUT IN LIFE EXPERIENCES
AND RELATIONSHIPS

As older adolescents assume greater responsibility for their personal lives, expand their circle of friends and acquaintances, and take on part-time jobs in the "adult" world, issues of justice that once seemed abstract may become very real. Prejudice or unequal treatment in the work place may, for the first time, be personally experienced or experienced vicariously in the life of a friend. Having parents or other trusted adults with whom to share stories and to help differentiate the "crummy" from the criminal in personal experiences can be a great benefit.

ACTIVITY 4. REASSESSING
FAMILY ROLES
AND RESPONSIBILITIES

As a family, keep track of how family responsibilities are shared at home (who does what, how often, how long).

After a month, evaluate what the list tells you about family roles and responsibilities. What criteria is used for deciding who does what—gender, talent, availability, desire, sharing the tough stuff evenly? Are family tasks shared justly? Why or why not?

Try out a new configuration of sharing tasks round home for a month or two, then sit down again to evaluate how well the system is working.

Young people's involvement in seasonal sports and extra-curricular activities often means that some months are overcrowded while others are thin on outside commitments. Reassessing family responsibilities on a regular basis can help keep everyone attuned to what is going on in family member's lives and create a bit more openness to "going the extra mile" with household tasks when it is needed.

ACTIVITY 5. MULTICULTURAL CONNECTIONS: COMBINING FUN WITH LEARNING ABOUT OTHERS

Use holidays and vacation trips to open up your family to different cultural and ethnic experiences. Select from the following ideas:

- Take part in ethnic festivals and celebrations in your local community.

- Visit a restaurant that features ethnic cuisine or celebrate an ethnic night at home, involving the entire family in deciding on a menu and helping with food preparation.

- Check on the availability of art shows, musical per-formances, and other local events that can expose your family to the customs, traditions and talents of the ethnic or cultural groups that make up your part of the state or country.

- Subscribe to magazines and periodicals that feature stories about people from different parts of the world. *National Geographic World*, for example, is great for the primary school set. A family subscription to *National Geographic* or a justice magazine like *Seeds* or *Sojourners* can fulfill the same purpose with older adolescents.

The more varied and multicultured their experiences are while still at home, the more comfortable children will be as they move out into the varied and multicultured society that the U.S. is today.

ACTIVITY 6. EXPERIENCING THE IMPACT OF INJUSTICE ON PEERS

It is difficult for young people to understand the impact of injustice on people's lives until they experience injustice personally or see its effects on their peers.

Investigate, as a family, the needs of youth living in residential treatment facilities in your community (drug and alcohol treatment facilities, detention and correctional institutions, residences for abused or abandoned children and youth, homes for pregnant teen mothers, etc.)

Discuss together the problems and situations that forced young people into these settings and how these same problems are played out in your neighborhood or town.

Talk with a social worker, chaplain or minister at one of the facilities about how your family can support one of its young residents through letter writing and visits or by responding to regular or seasonal needs.

Follow through on the contact.